SURFING PAYMENT CHANNELS

Expert Perspectives on "Waves of Change"
in the U.S. Payments System

JAMES D. PITTS

I dedicate this work to the thousands of professional men and women who work behind the scenes within the payment system, keeping the commerce of the civilized world in balance.

I give my sincere thanks to the experts who contributed their perspectives and to all the many others who helped make our thoughts and experiences into a finished product.

Table of Contents

Introduction

This book is about change in the payments system and the industry around processing payment and related transactions. The purpose of the book is threefold: to promote concepts, to inform readers (as users) of the various payments-system options, and to educate those who are interested as to recent history and future expectations.

The book shares over a dozen perspectives of payments-system leaders with differing backgrounds and roles in various areas of the financial-transaction industry. With so much unprecedented movement in the payments system, rapid technology development, and competitive diversity, change is inevitable. Consumer trends over the last few years are undeniable. Change can be exciting, but there is often a general resistance from those comfortably accustomed to long-term accepted methods. Add economic uncertainty, fraud challenges, change complexity, and costs, and the results are a myriad of options and mixed opinions—even confusion—on where it's all going.

This book will provide a single, safe source that many interested decision makers can reference to help them in the process. Readers will be able to access multiple perspectives from recognized payments industry leaders conveniently, on their own timetable, with no obligation, no sales pressure, and no social distractions.

As I said, I hope to accomplish three things through this work.

1. I want to allow notable leaders to share their experiences and promote ideas and concepts they would like to put in front of the industry and the public.
2. I hope to inform the readership about trends in the payments system that they would like to better understand or that they should at least be aware of. Ideally, they will be able to utilize the information to make informed decisions that will be valuable in their businesses or will better their lives.
3. I would like to take the second goal a step further and see the book used as an educational or training aid for individuals who are already involved significantly in the payments system as service providers or as significant users or for students who will be responsible for such things in the near future.

After twenty-five years of service within the financial-services industry, I hold near and dear the subjects covered in this book. With the passage of the "Check 21" legislation, I felt compelled to document the significant evolution we're experiencing in the payments industry. I hope others find it equally interesting and valuable.

Not being an all-work-no-play type of person, I couldn't resist the multi-pun title of the book. In some of my recent surfing experiences via television and remote, I came across a couple of good examples of the evolving payments system that I'd like to share with you to get you in the right frame of mind for further reading.

My first reference happened on a Saturday afternoon while I attempted to entertain myself through a seventeen-minute lunch break. My clicking remote paused on an old black-and-white western. The handsome gentleman from "back East" had just hit town, and his conversation with the attractive lady he'd just met went something like this:

"I'm planning to conduct a little business while I'm here. Could you direct me to your local bank?" the gentleman asks.

"I'm afraid we have no bank here in Dry Gulch, but perhaps they can help you down at the general store," replies the woman.

They make their way to the general store where, after introductions, the stranger says, "I was wondering if you might cash my check for one hundred dollars?"

The storekeeper reacts. "Check? Oh, I've heard of those. They're the latest thing with those big fancy banks back east. Let me see what I can do." The other store clients look at the stranger with awe and respect as the owner scurries around, collecting cash from various hiding places around the store. The scene concludes when he proudly exclaims, "You can write that check for eighty three dollars and seventeen cents!" That is apparently all the money he has.

A contrasting experience appears in a commercial that begins with a questionable-looking young man walking through a grocery store in a trench coat. He's sampling food and drink along the way while stuffing various items into his interior coat pockets.

As he exits the store, a security guard stops him. "Excuse me, sir," the guard says.

I'm thinking he's busted.

The guard walks over to a machine on the wall and tears off a piece of paper. "You forgot your receipt."

OK, there's not much realism in either of these situations, but I hope my sharing these anecdotes helps you enjoy the perspectives you're about to experience in *Surfing Payment Channels*.

On with the show! (Surf's up!)

Chapter 1

Navigating New Waters: Lessons of a Changing Payments System

Rich Oliver, Federal Reserve

In early 1974, fresh out of graduate school and recently employed by the Federal Reserve Bank of Atlanta, I had the career-changing opportunity to serve as a staff analyst on the Atlanta Payments Project—a collaborative effort by the Atlanta banks, the Federal Reserve Bank of Atlanta, and the Georgia Institute of Technology—to design and deploy an electronic, card-based point-of-sale system in the city of Atlanta. Amazingly, the technology was available over thirty years ago to implement such a system. While the funding was never acquired to implement the system, it was during this project that one of the key participants helped popularize the term "checkless society." This burst of visionary enthusiasm stemmed from the early advent of the ACH (Automated Clearing House) Network and automated teller machines.

As time passed and check volumes grew steadily, if not explosively, we began to talk about a "less check society," and eventually just stopped talking about it. Along the way, the industry came to realize that not all parties to a check shared the vision. In particular, both consumers and businesses embraced the check as a convenient, ubiquitous, and inexpensive way to make a payment. Over the years, banks and businesses alike made it even easier and cheaper to use.

Eventually, historically fee-based checking became free to those holding certain balances, and today they are almost universally free to all account holders. Check writers pounced on the opportunity to personalize the process by purchasing checks with a myriad of clever backgrounds, from puppies to flags to collegiate mascots. And as volumes grew, everyone shared in the cost efficiencies resident in growing economies of scale.

In fact, in the late 1990s, industry pundits estimated that 62 to 65 billion checks were being written in this country, and that number was still growing at 1 to 2 percent per year. It was at this time that the Federal Reserve, the nation's largest processor of checks, decided to sponsor a statistically valid study of non-cash retail payments. No such study had been done within the industry since 1979. Dove Consulting and Global Concepts Inc. managed the survey work, which began in 2000.[1] In late 2001, the results were announced and revealed rampant growth in electronic payments and a stunning revelation that annual check volume was only 42.5 billion.

Clearly, when studies are done every twenty-two years or so, there are bound to be some surprises. So it was with some anxiety that the Fed repeated the study in 2003.[2] The results revealed that check volume had fallen to 36.5 billion transactions and that, for the first time in history, electronic payments volume exceeded check volume. Finally, thirty years after the enthusiastic promises of the Atlanta Payments Project, one can see the possibility of a checkless or near-checkless society. In fact, viewing the electronic solutions in place today and the nascent experiments going on

---

1.   Retail Payments Research Project: A Snapshot of the U.S. Payments System Landscape, Federal Reserve System, 2002.
2.   The 2004 Federal Reserve Payments Study: Analysis of Non-Cash Payments Trends in the United States: 2000-2003, Federal Reserve System, 2004.

around the globe, one can actually understand how the vision can be achieved.

Why now, after three decades, has this long-promised change taken place? I would suggest we are experiencing a bit of a "perfect storm" of environmental factors that have accelerated the pace of change to historically unprecedented levels. These factors include:

1. The existence of important, enabling technology
2. Heightened competition
3. Rapidly changing end-user behavior
4. Changing economics
5. Important changes in payments rules, processes, and laws

Let us explore these more deeply.

Technology

Recent history has been laden with life-changing technology in communications, transportation, medicine, etc. In the payments space, the primary accelerant is clearly the Internet, with document imaging technology a meaningful second. While the Internet is now the railroad of much commerce and associated payments and payments-related activity, its effects go deeper. Its diverse capabilities, from e-mail to an information fountain, from simulcasting of sports events to long-distance telephone, from advertising to purchasing, have made it attractive to almost every demographic unit in our society. And in the process, a significant portion of our society has become comfortable enough with the electronics to make raging successes of new companies like eBay and PayPal.

Competition

The landscape of the Internet and the changing technology undergirding payments has led to the emergence of technology-savvy, non-bank players who have filled the gaps in electronic solutions and created viable, competitive alternatives for corporations and consumers alike. In some cases, these companies are competing with banks that have also stepped up their games. In other cases, banks are outsourcing key payments functions to them. But in all cases, payments users have been attracted to electronic solutions.

End-User Behavior and Economics

This dramatic change in user behavior is clearly, but not completely, generational. Young consumers rarely write checks, relying instead on debit and credit cards and online opportunities to conduct their business. Corporations have begun to look to payments as a way to reduce costs and improve availability of funds. The urgency for this move to efficiency has been heightened by the changing economics of payments as the nation transitions from paper to electronics.

The positive scale economies of electronics have been no secret for some time, but investment costs and extensive competition have kept margins thin. Historically, bank payments revenue streams have flowed from paper checks and the card businesses. But now, as check volumes fall, diseconomies are prevalent, and excess capacity is everywhere. But there is no turning back. Like it or not, the future must be electronics.

Rules and Laws

Finally, the change processes have been abetted by changes in the rules and laws surrounding payments. The National Automated Clearinghouse Association's (NACHA's) efforts to expand the use of the ACH for check conversions and one-time payments over the Web and telephone have opened new doors. Nearly simultaneously, Congress passed the Check Clearing for the 21st Century Act, also known as "Check 21," which, along with NACHA's check conversion services, has created a new world in which checks written may not be checks cleared.

The NACHA rules allow non-corporate checks received in remittance lockboxes and at the point of sale to be converted to ACH debits as long as the customer has been notified. Check 21 allows collecting banks and other intermediaries to convert any paper checks to an electronic image of the item for further collection.

These five environmental-change factors have created some serious new challenges for players in the payments space. In fact, they have created a great conundrum. Can we as an industry step up to the challenge of declining volume and simultaneously downsize our legacy paper infrastructure, manage new technologies, and invest in a myriad of new electronic opportunities? Moreover, can we do it in a way that makes some sense from a financial business case perspective?

The answers to these critical business questions seem rooted in the answers to another set of provocative questions about the shape and pace of change. Over the past thirty years, we have lived in a dream world where the volume of every retail payments instrument (checks, cash, credit cards, debit cards, and ACH) has grown continuously. Today, for the first time in history, we have a payments system in decline, and it is unfortunately, the big one—checks.

Simultaneously, there is growing evidence that another source of payments profitability, the credit card business, is also under pressure. This stems from a growing trend of consumers to roll up profitable revolving-credit balances into home equity lines. Once again, the changing economies demand changes in strategies and careful judgments about future investments.

While there are any number of questions to be addressed to develop sound longer-term payments strategies, the following constitute a "sampler" of provocative key questions, the answers to which will affect investment decisions and the pace of change.

Are ACH conversion and Check 21 solutions interim in nature?

In other words, will the presence of widespread efforts to truncate the flow of paper checks help to change user behavior and, ultimately, cause underlying check writing to migrate to electronic alternatives? In essence, the converted or truncated check transaction looks more and more like a debit card transaction when it shows up on the statement. In fact, ACH check conversions frequently show up in the debit card/ATM section.

If there is an agreement that these applications are conceptually interim in nature, the question becomes, "How long is the interim?" The staying power of the check, as discussed earlier, has been considerable, but the emphasis, as it pertains to infrastructure needs, has shifted from checks written to checks paid. As noted earlier, while ACH check conversion can alter the flow of remittance payments (absent corporate checks issued by companies who "opt out") and checks written at the point of sale, the Check 21 law allows any and all checks to be truncated by the collecting bank. In either case, the paying bank will never see the check pass across their sorters, through their dispatch area, and over their ground transportation networks.

The meaningful lifespan of these solutions depends on the rate of adoption of replacement alternatives. The 2000 Federal Reserve study revealed that as much as 35 to 40 percent of all checks written are for remittance payments. The electronic replacement alternative for remittance payments appears to be electronic bill payment, either via a consumer-initiated credit transaction from a home banking system or by a biller-direct model where the customer goes to the biller's Web site and uses a credit card or authorizes an ACH direct debit.

Nearly two billion remittance checks were converted to ACH debits in 2005, and industry estimates are that millions of bills were paid online. Most large billers are converting checks and sponsoring bill-payment Web sites. However, lower rates of adoption are typical down market with many, many smaller billers. This implies a rather long transition to electronic bill payment for this category of business.

However, there is growing evidence that the business case for Check 21 image cash letter deposits is changing rapidly. The average dollar value of Check 21 deposit item with the Fed has plummeted from $18,500 in January 2005 to $5,500 in January 2006. While large banks appear to be making Check 21 deposit cuts at lower levels, smaller banks appear to be moving rapidly to a "clear all" model built on the back of branch capture. In essence, these organizations have the opportunity to eliminate virtually their entire paper processing infrastructure, including sorters, encoding machines, and transportation.

Consequently, it would appear that it will take several years for online bill payment to exhibit high penetration rates. (In fact, some significant percentage of bill payers may not be "banked" or Web enabled). In the meantime, check conversion and Check 21 options will dominate and, in the process, open the door to substantially reduced infrastructure needs at paying banks.

The second critical venue for checks is the point of sale where the Fed study estimated 28 to 35 percent of all checks are written. The extraordinary growth in debit cards (from 8 billion in 2000 to 15 billion in 2003) implies significant reductions in check writing are already underway. Recent announcements by Wal-Mart and First Data Resources to promote the concept of a store-branded debit card that clears through the ACH may help to attract more users to the debit card through promotion by the retailers.

Meanwhile, NACHA's coming implementation of the "back-office conversion" concept will allow retailers still receiving checks to immediately convert the item from paper to ACH in their back rooms (as opposed to the current requirement to do so at the checkout counter), in essence, treating the cash register like a lockbox. Alternatively, as noted earlier, the merchant can also use Check 21 (perhaps augmented by bank-sponsored remote-capture programs) and will make that choice based on its bank's pricing and availability terms.

As a result, it appears that the number of checks written at the point of sale will decline more rapidly than checks written for remittance payments as debit card usage grows and conversion programs are enabled. And, as with remittance payments, many checks will be truncated and cleared electronically. Once again, however, the number of checks actually clearing as paper items seems destined to decline significantly and rapidly over the next three years.

In summary, there are meaningful, rapidly growing electronic alternatives to checks (debit cards, Web-enabled ACH debit systems, etc.) that could replace a large number of checks written in the foreseeable future. But even if that transition is protracted, opportunities are in place to truncate checks early in the process. Ultimately, this implies that the industry's demand for check-processing infrastructure will decline rapidly.

Unfortunately, if you are in the check-processing business, this is both a blessing and a curse. The blessing is more amorphous, but it lies in the move toward a more efficient payments mechanism (though not necessarily a more profitable one). The curse lies in the stranding and associated costs of significant amounts of legacy check infrastructure that will inevitably create short-term cost pressures. This leads to the second question.

Will financial institutions, in an effort to cover costs and incent end user changes in behavior, revert to customer pricing models that make sense in light of the "new payments system"?

Twenty-five years ago, most consumers paid per-item transaction fees (in the range of fifteen to twenty-five cents) for each check written. As noted earlier, amid the battle for demand-deposit-account ownership, some banks began offering free checking for account holders who kept average balances above a predetermined minimum. Then came the offering of free checking that has become the norm throughout the industry. More recently, banks actually began paying interest on free checking accounts. Simultaneously, free home banking, free debit cards, and discounts or privileges for free ACH transactions have also evolved. Assuming that nothing is freer than free, this all begs the question of whether it is time to start charging fees for paper checks again (or in an even more radical world, using fees to differentiate between various payments alternatives).

Strategically, one thing is clear: in the midst of watershed changes in payments, we cannot allow future electronic solutions to subsidize the retention of paper. Moreover, given falling margins, the increasing cost of paper cannot be funded from revenue growth. So, the question becomes, "Who shall cast the first stone?" I sense it will be the first institution that is strategically willing to lose at least one customer in the name of long-term efficiency.

It is my observation that the payments industry, when confronted with profitability problems, inevitably turns to cost cutting, as opposed to revenue opportunities, to resolve such profitability challenges. At the Fed, which is driven by the constraints of the Monetary Control Act, we have seen the need to do both. Interestingly, price increases that have totaled 28 percent over three years have, when coupled with aggressive cost cutting, resulted in substantially improved profitability. In other words, while some customers were lost, net revenue was enhanced, and the contrast between paper fees and electronic fees has grown to the point where true incentives are beginning to exist for adopting electronics. While the "wholesale" model of a central service provider and its customers may not be perfectly equivalent to a bank's retail relationship with its depositor, the general lesson may be food for thought. Clearly, we cannot afford to invest in a myriad of future alternatives in an environment of falling margins. Regardless, we will have to continue to minimize infrastructure along the way, which leads us to another important question.

Will the industry find ways to truly collaborate on issues of a noncompetitive nature, such as shared infrastructure, as a means of increasing overall efficiency?

At the risk of incurring widespread wrath, I think it is fair to say the most well-intentioned industry consortiums have failed to live up to their expectations. Perhaps it is too much to expect in such an aggressively capitalistic society, but it is bewildering to me that major players cannot find ways to share costs in a declining business like check processing. Certainly, the concept of sharing brings with it a natural loss of control over the shared resource, and inevitable sacrifices. But what better place to explore such options than in businesses that are declining (and, hence, have become commoditized) or appear interim in nature (such as Check 21).

It is for this reason the Fed and SVPCo are collaborating to reduce infrastructure needs for shared customers. It is for this reason that shared image archives make sense. Both examples ultimately free up resources that can be more effectively spent on competitive, future electronic services rather than on the last vestiges of the paper world.

Of course, all of this discussion implies the recognition of a seed change in customer behavior. The traditional idea that a customer's loyalty is based on the ownership of his checking account may need to be questioned. Today's young consumers clearly don't write many checks; in fact, they barely understand why they exist. Debit cards, credit cards, and online payments are their world. Customer attraction and "stickiness" are more likely to come from the convenience and "coolness" of inter-face technology. For many customers, loyalty is only awarded to the next gimmick in the marketplace. Consider the cell-phone market. Even I have owned three different cell phones from three different service providers in the last six years. This, then, leads to a final question for consideration.

Will we, in the payments industry, finally begin listening to our customers needs rather than building solutions that meet our needs?

In my recent experiences at a number of industry conferences, I have heard corporate America criticize the financial industry in increasingly strident tones for not listening to their customers' needs. They claim that banks are trying to push customers to adopt solutions that are good for rationalizing bank operations and maximizing bank profits rather than inventing solutions that allow corporations to reduce costs and improve operations.

Banks, in turn, counter with the argument that corporations do not understand the complexity and cost of the services offered by banks. While I would not dare to referee such a dispute (though I suspect the truth is somewhere in between), I would opine that the idea of more closely listening to customers has growing merit. If there are falling markets, and if there are multiple investment alternatives to be considered, the price for being wrong becomes more expensive. In other words, it is no longer viable to make dog food that the dogs won't eat.

This approach to being right more often implies a new commitment to customer sensing, product-life-cycle development methods, and rigorous business case analysis. All of this is directed toward enhancing the value for both the customer and the service provider and creating a platform of trust rather than a checking account on which to build loyalty.

A failure to do so opens the door to new, non-bank organizations to find places in the marketplace. Free from the shackles of tradition and bolstered by their adeptness at harnessing technology, such firms are rapidly finding profitable niches, providing value-added services, and leaving the tedious chore of managing account balances to financial institutions. While some may say this is unfair and others may proclaim that these unregulated parties are introducing new risks, it may be that this is simply the reality of the new world.

In fact, I may be so bold as to observe that many financial institutions, challenged by falling margins, may find themselves outsourcing various aspects of their payments businesses to trusted non-bank third parties as a means of providing a full range of electronic services to their customers. Further, absent any regulatory advances on these unregulated parties, the marketplace will likely "ensure" trust by evolving strong risk management practices and contractual obligations.

In summary, we have laid out just four of many questions whose answers will "in fact" affect the shape and certainly the pace of change. And change we will, for the die has finally been cast after thirty years of waiting. The years ahead will be no time for the weak or tentative; but a time for bold, calculating action.

To be successful, organizations will have to throw off the bounds of the past and focus on making wiser long-term investments than ever before; pass along changes in service levels and pricing to customers in such a way that supports the future, not the past; collaborate and share with other industry players in areas where sharing makes sense; and genuinely work more closely with customers to bring to market the products and services they truly desire.

These have not always been strengths for our industry, but working on our weaknesses is a must. In 1612, as Europe emerged from the winter of the Dark Ages into the bright spring of the Renaissance, Francis Bacon spoke some powerful words. "He who will not apply new remedies must expect new evils, for time is the great innovator." Bacon had no idea what was to come four centuries later. But he captured the essence of the threat we all face—change or become insignificant. It's time to change.

Chapter 2

Payments Observations 1960–2006

Jerry Milano, The Clearing House

Picking out significant payments processes or events over almost fifty years can be a challenge. Making them interesting to other people is probably more difficult. Clearly, some significant payments issues and events, bank cards, and wire transfers come to mind, but my direct experience has been siloed. Here's my top ten in the order I experienced them:

- Direct deposit and ACH
- Computers and online banking
- ATM proliferation
- Nine-digit routing numbers
- Fed pricing and settlement
- Check safekeeping and truncation
- UCC 4103(b)
- Electronic check presentment

- RCK, ARC, and back-office check conversion
- Image archive and exchange

As a high school student, I held a part-time job in a neighbor-hood savings and loan on the west side of Chicago. Branching was taboo in Illinois, and the association was hard-pressed for growth opportunities. The marketing strategy revolved around sponsoring the Chicago Cubs on the radio to build name recognition and selling direct-deposit savings programs to businesses by offering to service both savings accounts and U.S. Treasury savings bonds by payroll deductions. The combination of payroll savings and name recognition from the Cubs' games helped grow the S&L over the next six years. After college, my banking career moved to a large commercial bank that also ran a bank-at-work marketing operation. The hot new marketing ploy was to offer direct deposit to any bank account through the newly implemented automated clearing house.

The bank sales reps would target a company and offer payroll services to the CFO with free checking and savings accounts to employees that wanted them. The CFOs would resist the program if they thought their employees would have to switch banks, so direct deposit to competing institutions' accounts through the ACH turned out to be key to success. The bank made enough off the corporate account, payroll fees, and the large percentage of employees who chose free checking to make the program worth-while. As our marketing programs became more sophisticated, we learned that bank customers using multiple services almost never changed banks. Someone had to die or move out of state to cause an account closure for a multiservice client. We learned how to load features into the deals to increase account retention. Judging from the almost daily marketing offers in my mailbox, marketing strategy hasn't changed much in forty years.

The biggest change in my banking career came with computers. The S&L had bookkeeping machines at the start but later shifted to Burroughs Sensatronic (magnetic stripes on the back of ledger cards to remember balances and improve bookkeeper productivity). It outsourced to an IBM tape-and-tab card system shortly thereafter and then followed by "in-sourcing" to its own IBM system as soon as the bugs were out of the conversion. All employees (even students working part-time) were sent for computer aptitude tests and, if adept, offered jobs in operations. Class schedules and other interests restricted my direct experience to decollators, stuffing green-line reports into binder covers, operating Phillipsburg mail inserters for statements, and other entry-level functions. These experiences proved helpful later for redesigning work flows and business case development. New applications often require an understanding of which support services can be reengineered at what cost or time savings.

After graduating from the University of Iowa in 1967 with a degree in creative writing, I went to work for the First National Bank of Chicago (later Bank One, and now JPMorgan Chase). The environment couldn't have been better for a young trainee. As a large commercial bank, First Chicago used very sophisticated systems: online, real-time savings; an online customer database; and, later, digital recognition equipment to read printing and handwriting, to encode checks, and to automate proof. The bank's culture took these systems for granted as they were installed, and so there was very little awe except when visitors came to observe our operations. The growth rate of the bank and the acceptance of technology integrated into operations created an environment of almost perpetual change and little fear of failure on the systems side of the house. Older managers were more conservative. The multiplicity of systems at the bank created natural combinations of systems use that soon became second nature. Many people began thinking about systems integrations that would take the results of one system inquiry into another application. Some of the young guns wanted to connect everything to everything else.

It struck me that the young project managers were always complaining that the more-senior managers wanted to see the business case and the impact on customers, even when the benefits were "obvious" and even if the competition might install something before we did. The more-senior guys never seemed to get emotional and always asked simple, direct questions. And they always stuck to their guns, not approving a project until their simple questions were answered. It seemed obvious that the road to senior management was paved with direct, unemotional questions—a point that seemed to escape many talented project managers. It was also obvious that a little emotion didn't hurt when we were on deadline for a systems conversion. The project managers who showed up on Saturdays with boxes of doughnuts and coffee for the whole crew completed more projects on time and on budget than the guys who were all emotion from nine to five Monday through Friday but had more important things to do on weekends.

Systems integrations were especially complex. One project I worked on involved some of the first automated teller machines. As a management trainee assigned to retail banking tellers, I was initially interested in teller productivity. The downtown bank had lots of activity, especially at lunchtime. Unit-banking laws restricted tellers to a single building. The bank authorized ATM experiments as a way to increase capacity and efficiency by taking routine transactions out of tellers' hands. We also put ATMs into employee lounges so that teller capacity and retail lobby space would not be reduced with extensive employee transactions. Start-up problems revolved around electromechanical reliability and management fears of vending machine banking. A ruling that an ATM was not a branch by Comptroller of the Currency James Smith changed the thinking.

Illinois banks could not branch because of the unit-banking laws. When the federal regulator said that an ATM wasn't a branch, First Chicago jumped into ATM deployment with both feet. At once, the ATM became a way to reach out beyond the city block that defined the bank's domestic market. The only obstacle appeared to be risk concerns with offering ATM cards to a very broad user base. Online ATMs were a solution to the risk dilemma, but mainframe response time and reliability looked like a problem, as did development time for mainframe systems. The quick, low-cost answer was the minicomputer. A few years earlier, in 1972, we had developed a real-time mini system with dual processors, micrographic signature storage, and account balance verification. That system allowed our tellers to check customer signatures and balances and to hold funds when cashing checks. Connecting the ATMs to the same system (which occurred in 1975) allowed the human and the robot tellers to look at the same balances and eliminated virtually all risks of putting ATM cards into the hands of every depositor.

With the risk issues resolved, the team turned its attention to card distribution and ATM deployment; the bank-at-work program added company ATMs to the mix. After selecting companies that fit our profile for employees (tenure, average annual income, and remoteness of company offices from banking services), we offered ATMs in company offices as part of our payroll package along with the free checking and direct-deposit standard features. Several companies with 24-7 operations liked the program, and deployments began. At the same time, we launched a dozen "community offices" in locations with demographics that matched our metropolitan-growth projections. The offices were set up to do everything but take deposits or make loans. The ATMs took the deposits and the friendly neighborhood banker helped fill out loan applications and mailed them to the bank for approval.

It didn't take the local bankers long to run to the courts screaming about violations of Illinois's branch banking law. Our lawyers argued that a bank is a company that takes deposits *and* makes loans; our community offices did neither, and therefore they couldn't possibly be bank branches. We eventually lost the case. I learned that legal arguments sometimes don't matter. In big-guys-versus-little-guys cases, American courts usually favor the little guys. When the judge declared my department to be a violation of Illinois banking law, I decided to find another line of work before the bank downsized ATM operations.

A jump to the American Bankers Association in Washington DC looked like the best alternative. Not all states were opposed to ATM deployment, and ABA wanted some in-house expertise in the rapidly growing electronic-banking field. ABA needed an electronic-payments guru, and I had online teller, online ATM, and ACH experience in 1977. It seemed like a good fit; I took the job.

The next week, ABA's check expert quit, and my job changed from electronic-payments guru to payments generalist. A crash course at the Boston Fed gave me a rudimentary knowledge of check collection (from the Fed's perspective, anyway) and an interesting project: check digits on routing numbers and the amount field. I should have known that the change would involve more than just the mechanics of check collection.

Prior to my arrival, a joint committee of the Federal Reserve and ABA had studied the merits of putting check digits on the RT numbers and the amount field of checks. The Fed had done some internal research showing that if a check digit was present then erroneous entries could be corrected in processing by reversing the check-digit algorithm and inserting corrected digits in transit. While the task force had already made the recommendations, opposition in the banking community had arisen over the changes, with the lion's share opposed to putting check digits in the amount field. The major difficulties revolved around implementation of the program. The cost of upgrading proof machines to calculate check digits was one consideration. The logistics of reducing the amount field by one digit, actually putting check-digit generators on proof machines, and dealing with mixed-check-digit and non-check-digit amount fields in processing proved difficult to explain to the banking community. (It's difficult to explain today.)

The RT digit had been designated years before in wire transfers and ACH, so the elimination of the fifth-digit dash, the shift to the left, and the ninth as proof digit were predetermined. The amount field proved tougher; the proof digit was to be at the left end, not the right. The change would have required proof machines that calculated check digits on the fly, eliminating hundred-million-dollar checks (not necessarily a bad thing) and introducing the notion of automated amount repairs. Many banks were concerned about their liabilities for posting items that had been automatically "amount-corrected." Others were concerned that they might actually pay some proof-digited items at hundred-million-dollar amounts. In those days, Federal Reserve banks didn't take responsibility for processing errors, so an automated amount correction had different liability implications for a payer bank and a collecting Reserve Bank. The notion of an industry change over to intelligent proof machines at a standard cut-over date also appeared daunting.

At the time, it appeared like one more squabble between the Fed and large correspondent banks. I didn't have much involvement in the original research, but, by sheer luck and timing, negotiating the compromise with the Fed fell into my lap. Jerry McElhattan at Cleveland Trust gave me the winning argument, and I was glad to move it forward. Jerry pointed out that the benefits the Fed had calculated were industry wide based on the total number of checks cleared. When the benefits were divided out by the number of encoding machines, only the very largest banks could possibly save more than a half FTE with automated error correction. He pointed out that less than a half FTE was difficult to realize, and so the total actual benefits to the industry would be considerably lower than the original estimates. Ultimately, a compromise eliminated the amount-field proof digit and adopted the nine-digit RT. I'd been on the job less than two weeks, but I learned a valuable lesson: the Fed might actually back off a position if the opposing argument was fact based and well reasoned. The compromise accepted the nine-digit RT on checks and killed the amount-field proof digit.

The *American Banker* story reporting the nine-digit RT on checks named me as ABA's check-processing expert. It took some years for me to actually understand the expertise the newspaper awarded to me on the spot. In time, the nine-digit RT paved the way for all sorts of hybrid electronic-check-processing payments. It's hard to imagine how RCKs and ARCs would have functioned in the ACH without the RT number in plain sight on the original check. Some clever soul might have figured out an automated conversion process, but it would have added complexity to an otherwise simple process. That complexity might have been enough to drop ACH conversion off the radar screen.

The larger Fed issue in 1977 was, of course, Fed pricing. Overnight interest rates were at historic highs, and banks were dropping out of Fed membership as quickly at they could to grab state charters and invest reserves in U.S. Treasury bonds. Large banks were removing "national" from their names so that a shift to state charters would be available to them. The large correspondent banks worried that mandatory Fed membership with marginally free Fed services would put them at a competitive disadvantage to small state-chartered institutions with interest-bearing reserves. Universal Fed membership with free access to Fed payments would kill correspondent banking services. The Fed began to petition Congress for legislation mandating Reserve accounts. Over the next two years, the compromise came to be known as "Fed pricing," with mandatory Reserve accounts and fees for Fed payments services. What became the Monetary Control Act of 1980 defined the Fed payments services that would be priced. Key to the definition of priced services was defining settlement services separately from ACH, check clearing, securities collection, and wire transfer. The Fed lobbied hard for including settlement in Fedwire services, which would have knocked all private payments networks right out of the water since only depository institutions would have access to Fedwires. The final legislation listed settlement as a separate service from Fedwire, carefully preserving cooperative payments organizations like clearinghouses. Final Fed pricing was introduced at the beginning of 1982, about thirteen months after the Monetary Control Act of 1980 passed through Congress.

The battle over national settlement began almost immediately with the pricing announcement. While the legislation appeared to require it, the Fed wouldn't authorize national settlement arrangements. Private clearing systems had to restrict operations to a single Fed district or find a work-around. The regional ATM switches and bank card systems opted for national settlement using ACH entries. The process works but delays settlement by a day. That's not such a big deal when you look at the net values of POS and ATM exchanges. Even ABA's check safekeeping system (more on this later) opted for ACH settlement for truncated check clearing because multiregional settlement services were not available from the Fed. Multiregional settlement wasn't available for fifteen years until after Rep. Michael Castle called congressional hearings on Federal Reserve competition with private payments services. Pressure from the congressional hearings in September 1997 finally pushed the Fed to provide a national settlement service available to all payments services, but not before Bankwire and other private payments services threw in the towel.

As chief operating officer of the California Bankers Clearing House, I had the privilege of testifying in favor of equal national settlement services for private payments clearing services. I argued that the Reserve Banks should be forced to use the same settlement services as private operators since separate but equal never works. It didn't quite come out that way, but in 1998 the California Bankers Clearing House became the first check clearinghouse to post a multiregional settlement using the Fed's national settlement system. The New York Clearing House (later The Clearing House Payments Company) began using the national Fed service at about the same time for its ACH and CHIPS (wire transfer) services. Bankers Clearing House check services were acquired by The Clearing House Payments Company in 2004. Today, virtually all private clearing services use the national Fed service. Today, The Clearing House Payments Company is the only private clearing operator that uses the national Fed settlement for ACH, wire transfer, paper, and electronic check exchanges on a daily basis. Daily settlements are subjected to regulatory scrutiny due to their dollar value and are annually reviewed by KPMG under SAS70 guidelines. Ultimately, it is the range and depth of settlement experience that sets The Clearing House apart from other private payments operators.

During my move from First Chicago to ABA, the standard relocation travel package expired before I could get my house sold and move my family to Washington DC. My boss assigned me to help out on ABA's check truncation research project. I was assigned for two reasons: the ABA task force always met in Chicago to cut down the travel time for the research chairman, Joseph P. Coriaci, senior vice president and cashier of Continental Bank in Chicago, and I was able to travel to Chicago on research-project business to visit my family after the ABA relocation travel package ran out. I knew Joe casually from some Chicago banking social events prior to my relocation. As luck would have it, ABA's senior research manager took a job at Morgan Guarantee a couple of months before the research report was due for publication. I inherited the publication and the research project just in time to release the findings to the industry. While the research showed benefits from truncation, the major benefits were derived from replacing typical payer operations with what was called "bulk file–cycle sort" and from dropping the cost of statement preparation and postage if checks could be removed from customer statements.

The project involved forty or more large banks, all of which were interested in the potential benefits of eliminating the expense of transporting paper checks from one bank to another (hence cutting off or truncating the collection path). Digital imaging was the hot new technology to make it all work, and the cost-savings projections were enormous. We needed a way to explain to the industry that check truncation contained benefits, but substantial benefits could be derived from parts of the program implemented separately. Bulk filing was easy enough to understand; we coined the term "check safekeeping" to describe the removal of paid checks from customer statements and to distinguish that aspect of the program from the longer-term truncation at the bank of first deposit. We learned that "check safekeeping" was a term that better explained the process to consumer advocates too. We renamed the research project the "ABA Check Safekeeping Task Force" and announced a pilot test of end-to-end check truncation for any banks that wanted to try it with live checks. Seventy-seven major banks enrolled.

The toughest hurdle to launching the truncation pilot was the legal structure for the rules. We wrestled with the rules for months until a lawyer for the New York Fed, Ernest Petrikis (later, general counsel of FRBNY), invited us to lunch. Ernie said that the solution was right under our noses—that UCC 4103(b) permits clearinghouse rules to vary the code by agreement and that nothing in the definition of a clearinghouse required it to be a specific place. In other words, we could form what is now called a "virtual clearinghouse" and use the rules to manage the check truncation process. The National Association for Check Safekeeping was incorporated in Delaware as a clearinghouse shortly thereafter, and NACHA adopted special rules that allowed a truncated check (coded TRC, actually a precursor to ECP) to flow through the ACH. There actually was a bit of a battle at NACHA over allowing truncated checks to flow through the ACH infrastructure. Some ACH enthusiasts thought it would prolong the life of the check and delay the development of "pure" electronic transactions. It didn't hurt that Joe Coriaci had been elected chairman of NACHA just before the NACHA board voted to approve the check safe-keeping rules.

Once the rules were in place, we were ready to go, but we needed a way to identify checks eligible for truncation. The check printers jumped into the fray and suggested that there was an extra position in the MICR line, position 44, which could be used to create additional processing information on the face of a check. Unlike the ACH enthusiasts, the check printers rather liked the idea that the life of the paper check might be prolonged. The check printers petitioned the American National Standards Institute to designate position 44 as a process code field and the MICR digit "1" as the standard method to mark checks for truncation. ANSI readily approved the process, granting NACS the exclusive right to use the MICR digit "1" in position 44 to mark checks for truncation. Some check printers volunteered to make up test documents, the extraction software was tested, and the truncation process using the corporate dividend checks of the banks in the pilot were used to test the process. We wanted to be sure the banks were serious about truncation, so we required corporate dividend checks from the bank or its holding company as initial truncation items. We figured that if their own share-holders would be affected by the process, then the banks would be appropriately careful with the program. Initial results were posi-tive, although I left ABA shortly after the pilot started and didn't have a chance to track the project to its conclusion. I understand that NACS and the entire truncation project were subsequently moved to NACHA, and activity eventually dwindled to nothing;

NACS rules remained in the annual ACH rules publication until 2000, when NACHA dropped them for lack of interest.

While the use of UCC 4103(b) to simplify check exchanges with clearinghouse rules is fairly well understood today, in the early 1980s it was more of an art than a science. But the notion of private-sector payments operators competing directly with the Federal Reserve is much better understood now than it was in the early eighties when Fed pricing was in its infancy. NACS, as a virtual clearinghouse, became a model for two national clearing programs developed in the 1980s: ECP under the Electronic Check Clearing House (ECCHO) rules and interregional check exchanges under the National Clearing House Association. These programs have flourished, growing more and more popular over the years. ECCHO has evolved both ECP and full-image truncation rules. NCHA has been acquired by a large, regional, traditional clearinghouse and functions today as a national exchange vehicle, a regional clearinghouse, and an outsource provider of settlement services to small, independent clearinghouses.

UCC 4103(b) has also been used to introduce innovative practices into routine check clearing. Bankers Clearing House in California introduced a process in the 1990s that made the return of unauthorized documentary drafts identical to the NACHA process for returning unauthorized electronic debits. The rule was formulated after large California banks discovered that telemarketers that experienced large unauthorized returns problems through the ACH often turned to unsigned documentary drafts and then refused their return under the "midnight deadline" of the uniform code. The large banks argued that the consumer results ought not to be different based on the payments vehicle chosen by the telemarketer and that the consequences to the banks involved should not be different. The rule was adopted in 1995 at Bankers Clearing House, later written into the California UCC, and subsequently adopted by clearinghouses and state legislatures across the country. Most recently, the Federal Reserve has written the rule into regulation. In general terms, the rule allows a sixty-day period for the return of an unauthorized paper debit similar to the return period for an unauthorized EFT debit.

A more controversial use of UCC 4103(b) is the Texas Rule 9 adopted by the Southwest Clearing House (SWACHA, later NCHA) that allows the return of a check for alleged forgery. The controversy stems from the limitation on the collecting bank's warranty that the item contains no forgeries. The limitation is that the collecting bank will take it back for sixty days if there's money in the payee's account. The big "if" is, of course, the money-in-the-account requirement. Some argue that the warranty and the rule would be fine without the condition; others argue that the rule has been in place in Texas for more than ten years without adverse consequence. Whether Texas is representative is also subject to conjecture. Since this rule appears to fly in the face of *Price v. Neal*, the oldest court case in check law, there are almost as many opinions as there are banks. It seems unlikely that this controversy will be resolved anytime soon.

I've heard two versions of the start-up for electronic check presentment: the New York version and the California version. Both are true. In New York, some large banks thought that MICR read rates might be better if the collecting bank sent a tape of its MICR reads along with paper items presented. Payer banks could then verify their own reads against the reads of the collecting bank and correct items automatically without manual intervention. In California, large banks used to run transit items in both their northern California and southern California shops. They would find northern California items in southern California and vice versa. Since the items had already been captured, there was no need to repass the items; they could just run a tape of the transit items from the other end of the state and avoid rerunning the paper items in the posting run. Eventually, they figured out that the same was true of their competitors' items, and the practice of ECP was born. ECP was especially efficient in California because sorter time was most valuable early in the evening before the chartered jets left with their check cargoes. Replenishment values and reductions in reserves didn't hurt.

When NACHA put the Electronic Check Counsel together some years ago, the hot new subjects were RCK and POS. Some enterprising systems guys had figured out that return checks could be converted to the ACH and collected more efficiently than paper checks by inserting some intelligence into the return process (such as estimating paydays on the tenth, fifteenth, twenty-fifth, and thirtieth days of the month). The ACH purists were up in arms that the PPD code was not intended to permit converted checks even though the operators had put check writers on notice that returned items would be handled in that fashion and had received signed authorization to handle them that way. The tempest subsided when NACHA invented yet another transaction code for returned checks (RCK) and put consumer protections in place so that merchants could not return bad checks more than three times.

Merchants were also buzzing about the prospects for sending check transactions through the ACH instead of using debit cards. The merchants were complaining about the discounts they paid to networks to effectively guarantee the debit card transactions. ACH transactions at a few cents an item could be substantially cheaper than percentage discounts for credit and debit cards. Bankers were split between losing profitable card business and moving market share away from their competitors' bank cards. In the end, POP (point of payment) transactions proved to be too cumbersome to work effectively in check-out lines, and the entire process collapsed of its own weight. What emerged was the unobtrusive ARC (accounts receivable conversion) for checks at lockbox locations. Once ARC became the fastest growing part of the ACH, the POP folks decided that the back-office conversion of checks at retail outlets wouldn't be a bad idea and replaced the failed POP transaction with the BOC, essentially ARC in the back office of a store. The necessary element to ARC and BOC success was a Fed opinion that, despite the contrary text of the EFT Act, a paper check can be used to launch an electronic funds transfer through the ACH. (Such a transaction would be completely inappropriate if it flowed through any payments system other than one largely controlled by the Federal Reserve.)

Perhaps the most interesting electronic-payments phenomenon today is the image check exchange legally enabled by the Federal Reserve's Check 21 and approved by Congress following the events of September 11, 2001. Much has been written about the various aspects of Check 21. The remaining issue seems to be whether image network interchange or shared archives will prove to be the winning strategy in the brave new world of check images. Some want to argue that the volume of checks is declining at 6 percent a year so that there will be no need for imaging in ten years. Others argue that check reduction will level off in time and that images offer a lower-cost alternative to traditional check exchanges. At some point, even the nominal cost of swapping checks across the street becomes more burdensome than an electronic interchange of one sort or another.

The two camps seem to be the shared network and the shared archive. The shared-network camp, which includes my employer, The Clearing House Payments Company, believes ultimately that minimum network connections and overhead are the low-cost necessity and that no one really wants to be dependent on an outside supplier for the images necessary to customer service. Digital storage is cheap and getting cheaper.

The shared-archive folks argue that there really is synergy in large data banks and that, sooner or later, an industry-standard format will enable sharing without redundant images (the way shared archives achieve interchange today). Only time will tell which of the so-called industry-standard formats proves to be the one and only standard.

While it's a convenient opinion, considering my employer, I've never been a big fan of the shared archive; I've watched too many sharing deals between competitors unravel over the years. A shared archive is like a college roommate—interesting for a short period of time. Functionally, it's easier to share a network than a facility. For some period of time, the shared networks and the shared databases will likely coexist, but sooner or later the shared archive looks like it will collapse from its own weight. The shared-interchange network, however, can process transactions forever and never raise a peep unless it gets greedy in its rates or sloppy in its services. By their nature, networks are shared; networks connect endpoints. Absent greed or incompetence, the shared network can run for a very long time. Sooner or later, the archive roommates find too many value differences to peace-fully coexist. They part company on friendly or not-so-friendly terms.

Thanks for the opportunity to share a few stories.

Chapter 3

Perspectives on Check

James D. Pitts, Linx Payment Systems LLC

"I would like to begin by offering some food for thought. Here are a few fairly well-known pros and cons around paper checks in the payment system for your consideration before further discussion."

Pros
- Consumer (Check User) Comfort Zone

    The check is a familiar payment method that has worked well for a long time. It is widely accepted and convenient, leaves an accounting trail, and allows its users to participate in leveraging advantages allowed by the "float" factor.
- Universal Acceptance

    Businesses of every size typically trust checks as a payment form and have established methodology, systems, and processes around utilizing checks as a form of payment acceptance.

- Price/Cost

    The user expense associated with checks as a form of payment has been subsidized by financial institutions with float and other income associated with client relationships. As a payment option for consumers, the check has evolved from a fee-based service to a virtually free alternative in recent years.

- Proof of Payment

The check is its own receipt and is accepted as legal proof of payment.

Cons

- Geography and Transportation

    A check, as a physical instrument, is transport sensitive. The movement of the traditional check through the payment system is a physical event that requires extensive handling, transportation, and time. There are also border process and approval complexities around international and sometimes (even now) interstate check writing and collection.

- Paper Is Disposable

    Checks may be lost or destroyed easily and are not easily recovered without significant back-up processes in place.

- Fraud and Identity Issues

    With increased technology, fraud is an issue through forgery, counterfeiting, alteration, paperhanging, account takeover, and new-account fraud.

- Handling Costs and Risks

    At least two major expense items around handling checks have upward trends. I don't think anyone will argue about transport costs; we're all reminded of the high cost of fuel every time we fill up our car with gasoline. Checks are handled an average of six times or so in the traditional clearing process. Though highly automated, this handling remains labor-intensive and therefore error prone. Wages tend to move upward (look at minimum wage increases in recent years), and employee benefits are rising, especially if they include medical care.

The Business of Processing Checks: Cost and Volume Issues

As an executive director of a third-party check-processing service bureau, I had a favorite saying. "We lose money on every unit, but we'll make it up in volume!" OK, it's nonsense, but it expressed the reality that with volume growth it's easier to make the business case work.

Clearly, one of the issues around processing paper checks is cost. The world expects faster, cheaper, and better on an ongoing basis. As an industry, we've certainly done that when it comes to the art of check processing. In the largest check writing economy in the world, I enjoyed a long and interesting career managing check processing and remittance center operations. In a volume growth market, it seemed we could always imagine or invent a way to deal with the constant demand for improved performance and reduced cost. However, the volume turned downward at the beginning of the new century, and it has become apparent that significant change will be required to meet the world's expectations of faster, cheaper, and better.

On the tail end of the last decade's economic bubble, the expectations for growth and profitability seemed higher than ever. In the check business, however, even without the official numbers, it was apparent the growth just wasn't there. With what appeared and was later confirmed to be a shrinking market and with emerging technology that would likely eliminate or radically modify traditional methods of check handling, the obvious path to sheer volume growth as a third-party service provider would be to merge more banks' volumes together.

A great portion of my successes over the years were achieved by leveraging many smaller banks together to achieve economies of scale. I know from years of experience that this works well, and it can certainly be a temporary solution to gain efficiency during the industry's volume shrinkage. The technology factor, however, and new legislation that encourages taking advantage of new technology and opportunities that go with it will likely accelerate the change in such a way that the old paradigms likely just won't keep up.

For years, check processors have enjoyed the advantages of leveraging the volume of multiple banks. FiServ, EDS, Fidelity, and others have proved continuously that this type of leveraging works profitably and for the good of all participating. For almost as long, the vision of leveraging through cooperatives or consortia has been discussed and pursued but rarely practiced. Recently though, the trend seems to be picking up. SVPCo, Symcor, IPSL, and Viewpointe all seem to be proving the case. Cooperation to leverage volume can be a good thing. Cooperation and leveraging could prove a valuable alternative as volumes decline to help mitigate inevitable cost-per-unit impacts. Of course, like all other volume-based solutions, there will be a diminishing return.

It's unavoidable. In check or paper payment processing, there are fixed and variable costs. While you can usually reduce variable costs to keep up with volume losses, you usually can't adjust fixed costs equitably to keep up with needed reductions. In the growth world, we were regularly heroic enough to add 10 percent in volume with only a 2 percent increase in cost. Unfortunately, an operation that experiences a 10 percents volume loss and is only able to reduce 2 percent in expenses will be far from heroic as it becomes the first domino in a chain reaction negatively impacting their bank's financial performance.

Of course, even fixed costs are ultimately variable to those who plan and control the decline with extreme precision. Fixed costs could really be considered variable costs that simply have different extremes relative to volume sensitivity. For example in a twenty-million-item-per-month operation, it may take a loss of ten thousand items per month to reduce MICR ink cost, ten thousand items per night to eliminate the rent on a proof machine, and ten thousand items per hour to eliminate the cost of a reader-sorter or a portion of facility rent This is all taking place in an environment where the volume of the peak day every week is roughly double the low-volume day each week. Planning and execution while living this model will not be conducive to faster, cheaper, and better—at least not on a stand-alone basis.

Keep in mind, there are many more variables than just the volume decline associated with the writing of fewer checks. Even the future of this one category will be difficult to predict with all the options being offered in the new market and with the extreme shift from a generation of check writers to a generation that embraces the new digital world. Certainly, there have been and will continue to be huge impacts from new laws (such as the Check Clearing for the 21st Century Act), new technologies, institutional acceptance and direction, and the interaction of these dynamics.

Truly astute managers and institutions will accurately predict the impacts they can't control and manipulate the impacts they can control to make their "fixed" costs more variable and therefore less of a negative impact on their financial performance. If losing five thousand items an hour is intolerable to unit cost, then they will aggressively manipulate or rearrange the flow of another five thousand items an hour in the same time frame. This will be best accomplished by taking advantage of the changes in the law and technology to manipulate the institutional acceptance of check truncation at various stages during the check's life cycle. The general consensus, and I completely agree, is that the earlier a check is truncated in its life cycle, the faster and cheaper the process will become.

Certainly, there's a lot of consideration of consumers in this truncation movement, but I focus on institutional acceptance for a couple of reasons. Shear numbers indicate that it ought to be easier to coordinate change between twenty thousand parties than two hundred and fifty million. Second, as I mentioned before, consumers inevitably want faster, cheaper, and better. Faster and cheaper should be more easily attainable with truncation.

Institutional acceptance is generally based on betterment, or it should be. If this is done well, consumer acceptance should follow naturally. It's hard to argue with faster, cheaper, and better in this business—or any other, for that matter.

The ultimate opportunity to mitigate risks associated with unit cost increase in a production environment with decreasing volume might be a combination of cooperative volume leveraging and work-flow control by progressive truncation of paper checks. Many financial institutions are fiercely independent, however, and may feel they are capable of managing costs simply through truncation, work-flow improvement, or other methods without cooperative volume leveraging. One thing's sure: the tools and environment are more ready today than ever for effective electronification of check processing and clearing through cooperative agreement or check image exchange. One way or the other, faster, cheaper, and better should be on the way.

Quality Risks: The Paper Chase

For most people, quality is about service. I feel that way as a consumer. As a check and paper payment processing operations expert, however, I focus on three types of quality issues. The first regards customer service: you may lose your client if you can't keep up with the competition. The next issue is service accuracy and integrity. You'll be out of business or won't make money if you can't control it. The third is catastrophic-loss avoidance. Most people don't mix catastrophic loss into their thinking about quality, but I think brain surgeons, nuclear power plant engineers, commercial aircraft pilots, and large-scale check-processing operations should consider quality control, especially around catastrophic loss, as one of the most important aspect of their jobs.

To help you understand these three types of issues and the attention I'll give them, I'd like to remind you of my short list of pros and cons around the check as a method of payment and paper as a medium. Many of the pros, though valid, are weak in this day and age. Several of the cons put users at risk (my second quality issue) and have a potential for catastrophe (my third but primary quality issue).

My focus on customer service quality is strong. As the guy in charge of the back office, I had a tendency to gravitate toward the second and third type quality issues in order to avoid negatively impacting the customers (or customer's customer) no matter what. Of course, this obsession had to exist within the parameters of reasonable expense dollars. Regardless of this, there has been many an occasion when I, myself, or one of my associates in the back office actually invented and/or implemented changes that were all about improving obvious or highly visible customer service. In fact, this was a consistent priority. Nevertheless, there was usually a cost factor—our successful ideas usually also saved money—and, in general, most of the opportunity and responsibility for customer service "delight and dazzle" type quality was in the front office where the "customer facing" people worked.

A lot of time and energy in my career was spent addressing the second type of quality issue—if not proactively, then certainly reactively. When your profession is about what's in your client's wallet, and you're responsible for keeping the pennies accounted for, if you don't count right, then your client most certainly will. On a shortfall (and occasionally on an overage), you are going to hear about it, and you will be expected to make it right. Fortunately, there are a number of back-ups in most processes around check handling that usually allow you to address and correct a shortfall situation without having to make it up out of your own pocket or company profits. This is a good thing—especially if you're a third-party processor being paid about a nickel per check handled, hoping to make part of a penny in profit while taking over a thousand dollars in risk per check.

What insurance company would insure this type of risk, especially, when you consider my least favorite "con" from the list? Check payments usually utilize a disposable medium, paper, which can be lost, stolen, or destroyed. This of course is the basis for my focus on the third type of quality issue focus, avoiding catastrophic loss.

Not too many days after I "retired" from my position as a payment services operations executive, there was an accident in Dallas where a large number of checks were spilled onto a stretch of highway as they were being transported from the Federal Reserve to various local financial institutions. Of course, it wasn't the Fed's fault. The checks were being transported by a contract courier service. I became aware of the incident when I saw one of the local Fed executives on the news explaining the situation. I remember thinking, "Wow, it's great not to be on that hot seat anymore!" The highway had been closed off while clean-up crews hustled to recover all or most of the paper documents. The Fed executive carefully assured the public that the items were being recovered, that they had been processed, and that they were no longer cashable. She was right; except for privacy issues, there were no severe risks. The transactions were on redundant files elsewhere; the items were endorsed, or "killed," as we say in the business. I've been in that boat a time or two and in other similar circumstances. While it's never comfortable, it's not always a complete disaster.

In the early days of my career, I worked in Texas, which at the time was a non-branching state. This meant that for each bank I serviced, the checks to be processed usually came in from a single location. In a branch environment, those incoming checks arrive from many, sometimes several thousand, locations. Things were simpler then. The image technology of the day was micro-film, which is still used in many banks. Unlike the checks in the Dallas incident I described, these items were on the front end of the process, not the back end. In that environment, the banks always filmed and endorsed the items before sending them to my central site for high-speed capture, sort, etc. We considered this to be such an important issue that if work came in unendorsed, we considered it live (near cash) and locked it up, returning it to the bank to be endorsed and filmed before we would process the items. Today, in a time of massive branch banking across most of the industry, institutional practice and regulatory requirements can be very different; these can profoundly affect risk factors around paper as a payment medium.

My experiences with lost checks were often associated with one of several root-cause trends with fairly consistent outcome possibilities. Containers of checks can be misplaced when being transported from place to place. The cause may be something simple. For example, the shipper used a copier paper box as a check shipping container because it was a high-volume day, and they had run out of the usual cases. (This has happened more than once, I promise.) The courier then mistakes the box for copier paper and leaves it sitting by the bank's copier room where he always makes his daily pick up of the three courier containers and usually leaves the boxes marked "copier paper" behind. Another typical loss occurs when a clerk or operator accidentally throws checks away. It sounds like gross negligence for someone to throw thousands of dollars worth of checks into the trash. When you handle millions of checks in a day, the accumulation of rubber bands, plastic, cardboard, and paper is immense. Those copier paper boxes sometimes used as extra shipping containers on heavy days often become extra trash containers on the receiving end. They work quite well, unless someone doesn't realize they were a not-fully-emptied check container after they were a copier paper box and before they became a trash container.

After years of "dumpster diving" in search of lost cash letters, I can tell you that the copier paper box is not the worst enemy in this battle. Rather, it is the nine-day-old chicken bones you regularly come across when searching through the trash, which you retain for ten days as a precaution for just such an occasion. The good news, of course, is that when checks are misplaced, they are most often identified by an out-of-balance condition and recovered, assuming the institution balances on a current basis and escalates immediately when the condition is discovered. I'll point out that most operations send the bones, trash, and, occasionally, lost checks to the dump after a specified number of days.

A more serious incident can occur when the checks are not recovered. Again, it's particularly serious when the items are "live," or potentially negotiable. It's rare that misplaced checks are not found, but when a car or an airplane has an accident during transport, paper transactions can be permanently lost or destroyed. With this type of incident, or with any permanent loss of a negotiable instrument, a complex recovery effort can be created but may be partially unsuccessful. Flashing back to the non-branching era I grew up in, I can recall that even these extreme circumstances would likely allow a total recovery. It was tedious and had some associated costs, but with 100 percent redundancy via microfilm you were likely to recreate all transactions successfully.

However, as banks branched out into thousands of locations, the microfilm capability became a huge financial burden. Some institutions chose to encode, endorse, and film only in the centralized operations, leaving little or no redundancy in place from which to recreate lost items. My experience in these instances has been recovery of 90 to 96 percent on average. The larger the transaction volume associated with the loss, the lower the recovery percentage was likely to be. On a million dollar cash letter, that's a one hundred thousand dollar loss. While that amount is probably less then catastrophic for a large bank or service provider, for me it was a lot of nickels in revenue and pennies in profit that I had to make good on if the loss was deemed my responsibility.

On any given Monday night (or worse, a Tuesday after a three-day weekend), there are multiple check and remittance processing operations around the country processing tens of millions of items in a single location, some or all of which may have minimal redundancy prior to that point. If ten million items disappear, averaging well over a thousand dollars per item in value, you get the catastrophe. If 10 percent of those transactions are never recovered, that's over one billion dollars. That's tough for any errors and omissions planning to cover.

Please don't interpret this as a doomsday alarm or a push for resurgence of microfilm use. Believe me, neither is even remotely my plan or intent. Also, please allow me to emphasize at this time that a number of institutions still avoid this type of risk by filming before transport or centralization. Regardless, anyone in the business of handling financial documents is likely operating in a well-thought-out, prepared, and highly disciplined operation. I'm also compelled to guess that the odds of winning a lottery are probably similar to the likelihood that any of these mega check-processing operations will experience this type of catastrophe. In other words, don't close your bank account just yet.

The ideal process flow of a transaction initiated by a paper check no longer utilizes the centralized, mega-volume, well-leveraged, high-speed, paper-based operations that have served us so well in the past. As I think many experts already know and agree with intuitively, truncating paper in the check-based payment system as early as possible in the flow while simultaneously creating redundancy electronically will give us the most efficient, lowest cost, lowest risk check payment system we've ever experienced.

As I recall, risk of catastrophe seemed to be a strong factor in getting legislation designed to facilitate check electronification approved. Why then would risk of catastrophe coupled with cost savings (or cost-increase avoidance) not be a compelling case for moving forward as soon as possible to leverage to the fullest the opportunities provided by the legislation?

Where Checks and Other Payments Go Next (Not Next Week–Next Generation)

My guess is that the volume of checks completing their life cycles as paper payments will continue to fall steadily and perhaps level off temporarily at ten to fifteen billion annually (a popular prediction) in the United States. This leveling off may be for an extended or barely noticeable period but will inevitably continue to the level of virtual extinction. I believe we will most likely continue to see paper checks as source documents for several decades. However, the volume of checks being truncated at some point in the process and indeed the creation of checks electronically will eventually eliminate the paper documents running the full course of the transaction.

To address the comfort zone that has developed with the check as a trusted payment form, I'll have to admit that for a good period of time the check has reigned and may continue to do so. As for the paper requirement, its value is passing. Paper technology was the best technology readily available for a long time. It served well as proof of transaction, was difficult to forge, and was usually efficient to use. Today's technology has made paper more vulnerable than ever to forgery, weakening the paper check's value. Couple that with the cost and risk issues of paper, and electronic technology will inevitably win out. One of the chief ingredients that made the check so successful is still there, however, and will continue to perpetuate the value of the check as an electronic transaction. It is the same and only thing that allows any payment system to be effective when the transaction medium has less immediate value then the product or service it is exchanged for. It is the same thing that will be supporting all emerging electronic payment options. It is the integrity generated by the rules, processes, and performance and backed by trusted institutions like governments and banks. As physical entities, ink and paper are weakened by technological advances, and the growing trust in credit cards, ACH, and electronic checks will continue to grow. This is largely due to the efforts of institutions to generate and maintain payment integrity with verifiable process and backing (incurring or mitigating risk) of certain methods. It's also safe to assume that new technologies will be developed and applied to electronic-payment security as well on an ongoing basis as the popularity of electronic payments grows and demand for security improvements becomes higher. Among these, you're likely to find RFID, biometrics, and similar technologies.

In other words, technology has made or will make a paper check no better proof of payment then an electronic record. Both can be manipulated and forged. Financial institutions and governments will continue to improve process around emerging payment systems and in doing so will aggressively mitigate the risk of use. They will also accept liability for the integrity of their processes by accepting a portion of the risk associated with that use (as they always have). A good example is credit card liability limits for users.

Popular electronic transactions, including the use of electronic checks, will continue to grow. Physical check processing will decentralize as truncation moves continuously toward "point of creation," until it gets there entirely. There are significant steps between here and there, so don't confuse this with apocalyptic or immediate prophesy.

Will the check as an electronic payment reign in a similar fashion to the paper version? Who knows? I like the theory that all transactions become either a debit or a credit in some universally accepted medium, but I think that's a long way off. It's a little hard to imagine in any society that truly values diversity and choice as we do.

What about cash? It could follow checks or even go first, depending on convenience, privacy, and issues around tradition. Don't worry about guns and liquor though; they'll always be in demand—so keep collecting!

Chapter 4

A Short History of NetDeposit Inc.

Zions Bancorporation Vision

Zions Bancorporation, a Utah-based holding company for eight strong regional banks throughout the West and Midwest, is recognized as an innovative player in the regional banking area. Led by industry leading, out-of-the-box thinkers, Zions Bancorporation has grown to forty-three billion dollars in assets since its founding in 1955.

In recent years, Zions has also taken an active role in developing technologies with a mission to evolve and improve the way banking is done. In the late 1990s, a group of visionary executives at Zions recognized that check volumes were declining and that technology advances and market conditions would shortly converge to change the way checks are processed and cleared. They saw significant challenges for banks to contain costs, given the high fixed costs associated with large centralized processing centers.

Zions would come to examine the options available to help the transition from a centralized check-processing model to an image-based, decentralized check-processing model. The goal was to capture an image of the check at the earliest point in the process, whether at a bank branch or the place of business, to

speed up check clearing and eliminate the costly physical transportation of checks. Out of this initiative, the concept of remote
deposit capture would be born.

The Early Concept—Internet Banking

The year was 1998. The Check Clearing for the 21st Century
Act wouldn't be passed for another six years. At the time, most
bankers were consumed with a disruptive new technology—
Internet banking.

At the time, Internet banking was promising to enable the
demise of brick-and-mortar bank branches. This concept was
flawed in that people still wrote checks and the Internet had
yet to address a virtual check deposit process. This problem was
both obvious and troubling to Zions' CIO, Danne Buchanan.
While searching for a creative solution to the problem, he landed
on the concept of enabling retail banking customers to scan
check deposits at home and transmit them to the bank over the
Internet.

The radical concept had a few challenges. First, the industry
would have to accept an image of a check rather than the original
check for payment. And second, there was a shortage of check
imaging equipment on the market designed for small volumes.
The hardware that was available was cost prohibitive for a retail
banking customer. Initial market research showed that these
customers would require a scanner priced at fifty dollars or less.
Scanner hardware at the time was running in the range of two
thousand dollars per unit.

Then another epiphany occurred. What if such a service could
be made available to commercial banking customers? Given the
high dollar amount of the average commercial check, corporate
customers would likely be less price sensitive and could benefit
in many ways from such a service. This model showed more
promise, and Zions decided to develop the concept under the
leadership of Mr. Buchanan.

The Bubble Burst

As Zions began to work on this concept, the Internet bubble was about to burst. And when it did, the idea of Internet banking changed with it. Many Internet-only banks failed overnight, and others were merged into existing brick-and-mortar banks. The idea that the Internet would remove the requirement for brick-and-mortar branches also died. The Internet did prove to be value-added service to banks, and as customers adopted the technology, banks started to see the other benefits of Internet banking, including bill pay and online images of checks. The Internet also proved to be a catalyst for the remote deposit capture of checks.

Patent It

Great ideas must be protected, and Zions recognized that they had a great idea. So a project was formed to patent the concept. The patent application covered a wide range of concepts, including distributed item capture, rules-based item decisioning, electronic clearing mechanisms, etc.

The patent application has proven to be predictive of the market dynamics currently in play. Despite its early introduction and no defendable cases of prior art, the patent application remains in the U.S. Patent Office, awaiting approval.

Development for Zions—The First Remote Deposit Capture System

Through work on the patent application, Zions realized that the product concept was too good not to pursue. The benefits to its customers would be too great. So, in 2001, a team was assembled to develop a remote deposit capture offering for customers of Zions Bank. Again, Danne Buchanan was tapped to lead this effort.

Danne organized a development team and began building a distributed capture system, including what were termed a "remote client" and a "decision gateway" to receive the remotely captured items. This was the origin of the terminology commonly used in the marketplace today to describe this service.

Again, the issue of the high cost of check scanners came up. Danne began searching for a viable provider to develop the type of unit that could deliver the functionality required by Zions's business case. This led him to Italy, where he began what would be a strong relationship with the compact check scanner hardware industry. Eventually, a product line was developed that could meet the needs.

By early 2002, a working prototype of Remote Client had been produced. These remote capture nodes fed a decision gateway that was tightly integrated with the check system used by Zions Bancorporation's item processing operation.

It was at this time that Zions named the product line "NetDeposit." They secured a handful of beta customers to begin using the product. Initial beta customers included a health club, a food services company, a nonprofit organization, and Zions's own credit card group.

By obtaining approval from their customers with agreements, these beta customers began transmitting deposits via Remote Client and remote deposit capture was born. This was done before the legal underpinnings, Check 21, became law. In another bold move, Zions decided to use indemnification language on the image of the item and to treat the item as a photocopy of the original. This was a risky venture, but Zions believed in the concept and that the regulations and laws would soon catch up.

Check 21 Proponent

Check 21, a new piece of legislation being proposed by the banking industry, was well underway when Zions started sending its first image items. Zions recognized the opportunity that Check 21 presented. Nobody was more passionate or knowledgeable about the opportunity than Danne Buchanan. In fact, he was chosen to testify before the U.S. Senate in support of the legislation representing the American Bankers Association, America's

Community Bankers, Consumer Bankers Association, the Financial Services Roundtable, and the Independent Community Bankers of America. This was the first time one individual represented all of these varied interest groups.

Check 21 introduced the image replacement document (IRD). Danne recognized that the IRD was the catalyst for moving banks to check electronification. Because settlement involves two parties, image-based settlement would require the ability to both send and receive images. With the IRD, banks would be able to transition to an electronic workflow and move the electronic item as close as possible to the receiving bank before reconverting it to an IRD for presentment.

However, to fully unleash the value of Check 21 and negate the encumbrance of geographical distance, a nationwide IRD print network was required.

Introducing Remote Deposit Capture to the Market

To take NetDeposit to market, Zions needed an industry partner with enough nationwide geographic presence to establish a viable IRD ecosystem. Zions found a like-minded partner in EDS. EDS caught the vision of the NetDeposit system and committed to deploying an IRD print network based on NetDeposit software.

Seeing the value of what had been created and the value EDS could bring to the system, Zions quickly realized the value that the product would bring to the entire banking industry. While the product would provide a strong competitive advantage if Zions kept it to themselves, they realized the larger potential available by offering it to the entire market.

Zions reached a distribution agreement with EDS, who would host the NetDeposit technology for banks wishing to take advantage of this value proposition. With the EDS partnership in place and the IRD print network being built, Zions was poised to take NetDeposit to the market.

In anticipation of going to market, Danne looked into the Zions Bancorporation organization, including technology ventures, and hand-selected stars that had the unique combination of strengths necessary to build a new venture. Senior people with deep banking experience, technology know-how, and business acumen were brought onboard.

NetDeposit Inc.

In January 2003, with the team assembled, a promising new product line, and a committed partner, Zions Bancorporation incorporated NetDeposit and Danne Buchanan was named its CEO.

NetDeposit Inc. immediately began execution toward key goals. The first was to convert its software from a service internal to Zions Bancorporation to a licensable software product. The second was to find a marquee customer.

All of 2003 and most of 2004 were spent packaging the software product and supporting the system in production at Zions. While extremely difficult, the combination for supporting a live system and doing product development catapulted NetDeposit up the learning curve of what is required to deliver a successful remote capture system. By now, NetDeposit was running the third generation of software and building the fourth. In addition, it was gaining valuable experience in deploying and supporting the scanner hardware element of a remote capture system. This experience has proved to be invaluable in delivering a solution that can scale to meet the needs of the industry.

NetDeposit went through its first branding exercise, renaming the remote deposit capture software "Remote for Business" and keeping the name "Decision Gateway" for the virtual sorter (another term the company had coined).

A Crazy Idea

Throughout 2003 and 2004, NetDeposit spent a good amount of time evangelizing the concept of remote capture and using its business-rules-driven Decision Gateway to sort items to a variety of electronic endpoints and mechanisms. The idea of allowing anyone outside of the item processing shop to scan checks, deposit them to the bank over the Internet, and then electronically sort and clear them via image replacement documents, the Automated Clearing House Network, or image exchange was scoffed at—especially image replacement documents. "They are messy, costly, and risky," most in the industry were saying, but NetDeposit by that time had printed millions of IRDs that ran so clean through the check-clearing system that they were virtually indistinguishable from the original paper items

Prior to this, many banks had been converting to image-based check-processing systems in anticipation of a movement toward an image-based check clearing and settlement model, image exchange. While image exchange had not yet become the prevalent form of clearing, bankers were becoming comfortable with the idea of image-based check processing and were finding other operational improvements available through the electronification of items.

This had been done in conjunction with a consistent drive toward the consolidation of item processing operations centers for efficiency gains. At the time, any suggestion of reversing the trend and widely distributing check capture was considered preposterous.

Additionally, detractors did not understand how banks would seriously consider printing IRDs when image exchange offered such a superior, elegant alternative. And surely, the widespread adoption of image exchange was right around the corner—right where it had been for the last fifteen years.

Danne Buchanan and other NetDeposit executives were persistent in the face of skepticism, doubt, and, at times, ridicule. However, slowly but surely, industry visionaries began to listen and understand the vision.

Going for the Big Fish

Many new ventures go to market by picking a small customer, trying the concept, establishing a base of support, and then moving up market. Danne Buchanan rejected the strategy, recognizing that the banking industry looks to the biggest players and follows their lead. So, NetDeposit chose to pursue the biggest customer they could find. The target was Bank of America.

NetDeposit recognized that Bank of America was the clear market leader in setting trends for others to follow. NetDeposit and EDS assembled a team completely dedicated to selling to Bank of America. Together, they pitched the concept to Bank of America, who, as expected, immediately saw the value. Bank of America signed on to the service.

NetDeposit then set its targets on the top fifty banks in the country and other industry leading service providers.

Maturing the Technology and the Company

Through its interaction with Zions, Bank of America, EDS, and other large customers that had signed on, NetDeposit began maturing its products. Meeting the demands and consuming the feedback of the biggest, toughest customers in the market forced NetDeposit to completely dedicate itself to supporting them.

This interaction, though very painful at times for a small organization, forced the company to quickly mature its products. Dramatic improvements in performance, scalability, security, and usability were attained. In addition, NetDeposit expanded its scanner hardware fulfillment and maintenance functions required to meet the deployment needs of its customers.

Simultaneously, the company began to assemble a team of senior managers with deep backgrounds in the banking technology industry. Together with the existing bench strength in the company and the new talent, NetDeposit undertook the maturation of the company into a solid organization capable of meeting the needs of its customers. To better represent its product set, NetDeposit branded its products under the names NetCapture and NetConnect.

The C21 Marketplace Emerges

Check 21 went into effect on October 28, 2004. Even as this was happening, NetDeposit was predicting the emergence of a new marketplace dynamic that it termed the "C21 Marketplace." NetDeposit could see that the combination of the new rules and new technology would create a disruptive environment where geography would no longer matter, and banks could actually move market with distributed capture technologies.

The new landscape would be more competitive than ever, and new rules of engagement for banks would be introduced. Financial institutions would not only fend off existing competitors located in their geographic region but also protect their current corporate customer accounts from financial institutions found hundreds or thousands of miles away. Banks that would not acknowledge the changes in the market environment, actively participate in the C21 Marketplace, and determine how to leverage new business opportunities would find themselves at a great disadvantage. Relying on old thinking, old technologies, and old products was a formula for failure.

NetDeposit continued to promote this prediction through 2005 and into 2006. In 2005, the industry began to wake up to the successful deployment of distributed capture and electronic clearing technologies by forward-thinking banks. And, true to NetDeposit's prediction, these organizations began to actually win customers from both inside and outside of previous geographic limits.

Starting in 2005, the market uptake of the technology began heating up. Aggressive banks began selecting and implementing a world-class, robust system they could use to win business from competitors. Others took a more timid approach, implementing low-tech defensive products. A third category chose to sit out of the game, opting to ignore the trend or "wait and see."

Staying Ahead of the Pack

Since its inception, NetDeposit has led the field in the development of image-based, distributed payment capture technology. NetDeposit was first to market with a corporate remote deposit capture platform, an image-based "decision gateway" for sorting and routing electronic items and large-scale image-replacement-document (IRD) print software. This technology has been matured over several generations of development and through direct feedback from customers running systems in production.

For over four years, NetDeposit technology, in production, has enabled remote capture and electronic clearing and currently powers the nation's top IRD print networks. NetDeposit solutions have processed millions of electronic items. NetDeposit offers its technology under license agreements or as an outsourced service through its innovative NDpro Managed Services business line.

With its experience and success, NetDeposit continues to innovate to stay ahead of the pack. The market has woken up to the opportunity. The same concepts NetDeposit was once ridiculed for are now at the heart of its competitors' product strategies. While NetDeposit has been able to leverage its significant experience meeting customers' needs into market leading products and services, it continues to peer into the horizon, looking for the next market direction.

NetDeposit's business strategy is to help its customers win the C21 Marketplace and take full advantage of Check 21. This means providing the complete set of products and services required for organizations to take advantage of new rules and technologies in order to dominate new markets. Doing so places NetDeposit's business strategy squarely in the middle of new payments technology space with a focus on providing powerful distributed capture technologies and the tools to manage the resulting electronic workflows.

Chapter 5

Check Clearing House Role in an Evolving Industry

Glenn Wheeler, NCHA

The check clearinghouse in the United States traces its roots as far back as the late 1800s. The history of the National Clearing House Association (NCHA) dates back to 1890. Since then, check clearinghouses have evolved significantly from their humble origins as mere meeting places for financial institutions in a common geographical area to exchange paper checks deposited by their customers that were drawn on other local financial institutions.

How do financial institutions benefit from a clearinghouse? They benefit by having the ability to directly exchange checks that are drawn on each other as opposed to paying an intermediary such as the Federal Reserve Bank to deliver and settle the dollars. In addition to exchanging the physical items drawn on each other, financial institutions also settle the dollars for the total amount of the dollar value for all the items exchanged. This process permits financial institutions to pay (debit) for checks they receive and are paid (credited) for checks they present to others. The identification of the total dollar values exchanged and the posting of the related entries are referred to as "settlement."

The settlement process has experienced its greatest evolution in the last twenty years. Dating all the way back to the late 1800s, clearinghouses used manual tally worksheets to chart dollar totals that were being exchanged during a given period of time. With the invention of the computer, standard spreadsheet software began to replace the handwritten form.

Photo of the original record book from 1890
framed and housed in the NACHA's Houston office.

By the 1990s, a few clearinghouses began to look at more sophisticated computer programming, utilizing database capabilities to provide reporting tools to assist financial institutions in balancing and reconciling the checks they exchanged with each other. The formation of the National Clearing House Association in 1992 expanded the concept of the local check exchange to a national level. The explosive growth caused by this expansion across the United States created new challenges that required a more advanced settlement program.

The NCHA was the first to incorporate the concept of a local check exchange into a national format. Rather than having a central meeting point, such as those existing in local clearinghouses, checks were now physically transported from the presenting financial institution to the receiving institution. The collective dollars were then net settled using a settlement process created by NCHA. Checks were delivered or exchanged over long distances via air transportation.

The unpredictable timing of delivery suddenly had much greater consequences with a national exchange where the distances checks were traveling increased drastically over local exchange routes. Gone were the days when financial institutions could simply use ground transportation, covering short distances to a common exchange location. Checks did not always arrive at their destinations at the scheduled time. Factors such as air traffic delays, weather, and aircraft mechanical issues increased the likelihood that checks might not arrive at appointed destinations by the required deadlines.

Increasing demand for real-time exchange and simultaneous technological advances ultimately led NCHA to develop the first Web-based, real-time settlement system, one that took advantage of the exciting, new capabilities offered through the Internet.

In the late 1990s, additional advances occurred within the Federal Reserve, beginning with the development of a product still in use today known as Net Settlement Service (NSS), which provides real-time posting capability of the dollars settled each day. With Net Settlement, members in a specific clearinghouse mutually exchange checks on a daily basis. The dollar totals are calculated using a settlement system that provides reconciliation-based reporting to the institutions. The settlement system calculates the dollar totals to derive a net settlement number for each participating institution. The clearinghouse then sends this number to NSS, where posting occurs to the institution's authorized account. The full NSS process is outlined in detail in the Federal Reserve's "Operating Circular 12."

Today, institutions exchanging checks on a national level can instantaneously see the dollars they are exchanging with other institutions that participate in NCHA. The decisions to "confirm" or "deny" can be monitored online simultaneously in real time by both trading institutions. Adjustments for incorrect dollar totals, returned checks, and reasons for returning checks, such as insufficient funds or closed accounts, can be immediately viewed online through a system such as the one NCHA manages.

Volunteer Versus Staffed

Most local check clearinghouse organizations do not have a full-time, dedicated staff; instead they are managed on a volunteer basis by staff within the participating member institutions, typically referred to as "members." The members often elect officers to hold positions such as president, secretary, and treasurer for a specific term of service. These positions are unpaid, and usually no single member institution may have multiple individuals holding office. Check clearinghouses are typically designated not-for-profit. Their existence is solely to provide services for members at cost. Members pay dues to the clearinghouse to cover those costs. In some cases, however, local check clearinghouses do maintain a full-time staff. For example, the Central Oklahoma Clearing House Association (COCHA), based in Oklahoma City, is an example of a fully staffed clearinghouse focused considerably on paper check and image exchange. COCHA also provides additional services to its membership, with an emphasis on risk management programs.

Some regions of the country have combined check clearinghouse functionality with automated clearinghouse (ACH) associations. Two current examples are Payments Resource One, based in Phoenix, Arizona, and Mid-America Payment Exchange, based in Kansas City, Missouri. These associations have full-time, dedicated staffs that are responsible for the local check exchange but also manage regional ACH needs for their membership. These needs include training, education, risk management, ACH rules interpretation, and other activities related to ACH transactions.

The Clearing House (TCH), based in New York, offers check clearing as well as ACH services. In additional to similar services offered by ACH associations, TCH offers ACH processing of transactions and operates a large wire transfer service known as Clearing House Interbank Payments System (CHIPS).

In October 2001, NCHA and the Clearing House Association of the Southwest (CHAS) merged and became the largest staffed check clearinghouse in the United States in terms of dollars and number of checks settled each day as well as for the number of exchanges for which it provides settlement. Focused on check exchange, NCHA also developed a national risk management program, focused primarily on efforts to curtail activities related to check fraud.

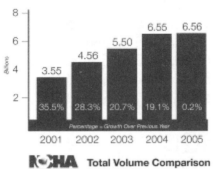

NCHA Total Volume Comparison

The introduction by NCHA of the real-time, Web-enabled settlement system greatly enhanced the efficiency for all users. One of the most critical components was the introduction of reporting tools necessary to balance and reconcile accounts related to the net settlement entry made through the Federal Reserve NSS process. The Web-enabled platform provided real-time access to reporting through direct Internet access. Users were not required to install software programs at their sites in order to access information since all necessary reporting could be obtained via the Internet-based settlement system through secure login and password access.

Security of data, ease of access, comprehensive business continuity, and reporting tools became significant benefits for participants within NCHA. Benefits of this settlement system became so widespread that other local and regional check-clearing exchanges desired similar functionality for their exchanges. Often, this interest came from NCHA members who, in addition to participating in NCHA member exchanges, also participated in other local and regional clearinghouse exchanges. Seeing the value of this settlement system, many clearinghouses agreed to contract with NCHA for settlement services.

Under these agreements, many local and regional clearinghouses contracted with NCHA to utilize their settlement system, with NCHA staff providing operational support. For these clearinghouses, this opportunity provided the ability to utilize a comprehensive system with dedicated staff without incurring the cost of developing and maintaining the application independently. As of December 2005, twenty local and regional clearinghouses have entered into agreements with NCHA to access the application. Additionally, two more clearinghouses in Nevada and the Pacific Northwest have merged into NCHA, becoming a part of the NCHA member exchanges.

Introduction of Check 21

On October 28, 2003, a historic step was taken in the world of check processing. President George W. Bush signed the Check Clearing for the 21st Century Act (commonly referred to as Check 21). Effective October 28, 2004, the legislation intended to facilitate check truncation without mandating receipt of checks in an electronic format. The act addresses this issue by creating a new negotiable instrument called a "substitute check." By providing this new instrument as the legal equivalent to the original check and requiring receiving institutions to receive the substitute check, if presented, Bush removed a major industry hurdle in advancing the inevitable progress of image exchange.

Financial institutions exchanging checks with other institutions could now electronically forward data and images (with no reliance on the original) of checks drawn on institutions capable of receiving them. For those institutions that could not receive in this manner, substitute checks could be printed at sites in close geographic relationship to the paying institution.

The elimination of the reliance on the original paper check removed the dependence on its transportation, thereby eliminating or reducing excess transportation costs. Additionally, through the utilization of this technology, checks are now presented more quickly, which reduces the sending bank's float exposure.

So how does this significant change impact clearinghouses?

The answer to this is somewhat mixed. Traditional check clearinghouses have historically been focused primarily on exchanging paper checks within a geographic area, with NCHA being the broadest interpretation of this through its provision of non-local check exchange under one net settlement. The ability to exchange images electronically removes geography as a key component. Regional and national financial institutions now view their trading relationships from a far broader perspective.

For example, two national banks that have items to exchange with each other would, in a paper exchange environment, potentially exchange this volume utilizing multiple local, regional, and national clearinghouses. In an image exchange environment, checks would be settled bank to bank without the geographical component that exists in paper exchanges.

To take this example further, if the two banks were to share a common image archive, the checks would not need to be "exchanged" but instead would be shared through access within a common shared archive.

The evolution of both image exchange and image share will ultimately reduce or in some cases eliminate the need for local or even regional clearinghouse exchanges. The migration will be to national exchanges that provide the greatest number of exchange relationships for the lowest possible cost.

Although there are significant changes for the industry in moving to image technology pointing toward image exchange and image sharing, one constant from the paper exchanges to image exchanges is settlement. Whether through paper or image exchange, financial institutions must have the ability to settle net dollars. NCHA, which already has in place a secure, trusted, broad-based settlement system, provides the industry with a national settlement platform that greatly assists the industry as it migrates from paper to image.

Partnerships

Historically, there has been no great need for check clearing-houses to engage in partner relationships with non-financial institutions. Check 21 and image exchange has created a new set of dynamics, which now make partnerships essential for clear-inghouses to provide additional value for their memberships and for the industry as a whole.

NCHA has developed significant partnerships with leading organizations to bring progressive Check 21 and image solutions to the industry. For example, NCHA has partnered with two major image solution providers, Endpoint Exchange and Viewpointe, to provide settlement for each organization's network.

Endpoint Exchange is the network that first brought to market items being exchanged fully through image exchange with no original paper requirements, a strictly electronic exchange of data and images. Participants on Endpoint Exchange operate similarly to any other clearinghouse exchange, with the important distinc-tion of eliminating geographic and operational hurdles that exist in paper exchanges.

With Endpoint's image exchange, checks do not need to be transported to a centralized or designated physical location. The ability to exchange in a virtual environment means there is no paper check transportation requirement, thereby eliminating transportation costs and accelerating the time in which checks present to the receiving institution.

Operationally, in an Endpoint Exchange environment there is no need to justify a particular send to a member exchanging in the Endpoint network. For check clearing analysis purposes, all the participating institutions can be analyzed as a collective commingled presentment. This contrasts to a paper exchange where checks are required to be sorted individually to each member participating within a clearinghouse.

With NCHA's technology added to the mix, the partnership permits the automation of settlement information to arrive directly from Endpoint Exchange into the NCHA Settlement System. Again, this process contrasts with the exchanges in a traditional clearinghouse, where each participating institution is responsible for submitting settlement information related to the checks presented to other participating clearinghouse members. Endpoint's settlement information submission process is more efficient and maintains the consistency of settlement reporting that is available for all NCHA settlement system exchanges.

The second major partnership involves the relationship between Viewpointe and NCHA. The Viewpointe model takes advantage of the shared archive approach. Through its shared archive customer base, Viewpointe's archive houses more than 50 percent of the checks written in the country. Viewointe has successfully placed into production a product known as ImageShare™. In this model, images warehoused in the Viewpointe archive are shared between the sender and receiver of the checks. Viewpointe owner institutions have publicly committed to using Viewpointe to share this common volume. Among the shared archive users, anywhere from 4.2 to 4.4 billion checks a year are common, or able to be shared, on the archive. Viewpointe, like Endpoint Exchange, has not historically been involved in settlement. With the partnership with NCHA, Viewpointe institutions that are members of NCHA now have access to NCHA settlement for any checks shared on the archive.

Another of Viewpointe's products, Pointe2Pointe™, allows institutions on the archive to exchange check images and items with other institutions not on the archive. This product features a networked image exchange model since the relationship extends to institutions not common to the archive, leveraging exiting Viewpointe connectivity to broaden exchange relationships. Again, participants in this product utilize NCHA for the settlement of those dollars exchanged via Pointe2Pointe™.

Both Viewpointe and Endpoint Exchange were successful in attracting institutions to their respective models. Endpoint Exchange generated participation from non-Viewpointe archive institutions and attracted the participation of thousands of institutions. As mentioned previously, those institutions common to the archive preferred Viewpointe's model. Although both organizations were successful independently, greatly increased benefits have resulted from the two networks' new interoperability.

The connectivity between Endpoint Exchange and Viewpointe became accessible to the industry in November 2005. The agreement between Endpoint Exchange and Viewpointe put into production the first interoperable connectivity of its kind within the industry. Critical to establishing this connectivity was that both Endpoint Exchange and Viewpointe utilized common industry rules and standards. Additionally, both organizations used a common settlement platform, NCHA.

The role of NCHA in the Endpoint Exchange/Viewpointe interoperability initiative demonstrates how partnerships are not only critical to the future of clearinghouses, but also accelerates opportunities for the industry to transition to a more efficient process of exchange.

Another instance in which NCHA has extended partnership opportunities is collaboration with the Electronic Check Clearing House Organization (ECCHO) for rules coverage for the items exchanged electronically. ECCHO rules are the industry standard for electronic exchange. Through the ECCHO/NCHA partnership, members have the assurance of the most comprehensive rules coverage both for exchange rules (ECCHO) and settlement rules (NCHA) that are available to the industry. All NCHA member image exchanges fall under NCHA rules for settlement and ECCHO rules for exchange.

Additional partnerships with NCHA include major check-processing organizations such as Fiserv and Jack Henry that further expand exchange opportunities for NCHA members and offer the ability to exchange electronically for the check-processing organization's clients. By outsourcing check-processing services, these institutions gain the ability to participate in a virtual exchange world utilizing the newest products. Through the partnership, trading relationships between NCHA members and the check-processing provider's clients became possible for the first time.

Since 2003, creating innovative partnerships has become a focal point for NCHA. Teaming with key industry organizations ensures that NCHA will continue to expand on its check settlement role in serving the industry.

Risk Management

Member institutions within clearinghouses have long been concerned with risk related to fraudulent checks. Initiatives have formed within clearinghouses on programs designed to combat the losses financial institutions have historically experienced through check fraud.

One prominent initiative to counter losses associated with check fraud generated out of Clearing House Association of the Southwest (CHAS), formed also in 1992 by the mergers of the Houston Clearing House Association, the North Texas Clearing House Association, and, a short time later, the San Antonio Clearing House Association. Most commonly known in the industry as Rule 9, the Check Fraud Warranty Rule was designed to combat losses typically experienced by the payer bank for items that were determined to be counterfeit. Under check law, payer banks have a requirement to return a check to the bank of first deposit prior to midnight of the day after presentment. If not identified through an inspection of the signature on a check by someone at the payer Bank, a counterfeit item is typically not discovered until after it is too late to be returned under existing check law.

Member institutions in CHAS made the determination that the innocent party in the transaction (the payer bank) should not be left with the loss associated with these items. Instead, the real party that should be held accountable is the customer of the bank of first deposit. It was this customer that initially accepted the counterfeit check and provided value for which the check was written. Additionally, it was the customer of the bank of first deposit that had the opportunity to verify the writer of the check was indeed that individual whose signature was on the check.

With this in mind, CHAS created a rule to modify the return timeframe for items exchanged between CHAS members that were determined to be counterfeit. By expanding the return timeframe, the payer bank could then, by rule, return counterfeit checks back to the bank of first deposit for charge back to its customers' accounts. Under Regulation CC, clearinghouses have a unique ability to modify check law by clearinghouse rule provided the rule is agreed to by the clearinghouse members. Important to note is that the only checks covered would be those exchanged by the members in the clearinghouse. Additionally, disclaimers were put in place so as not to simply pass a loss from payer bank to the bank of first deposit, but rather to get the loss completely out of the banking system. A common disclaimer is a sufficiency-of-funds test. If the bank of first deposit receives a claim from a payer bank but does not have sufficient funds to charge back the check to its customer, the claim can be disclaimed.

The Check Fraud Warranty Rule has spread from its origination in CHAS to other clearinghouses throughout the country, as well as being carried over into NCHA following the merger with CHAS.

Efforts around the expansion of the Check Fraud Warranty Rule demonstrate the role clearinghouses can play in addressing concerns common to its members. NCHA has built on this success by developing a comprehensive program for addressing the risk management needs within the industry. Now, more than ever, financial institutions are concerned about risk and fraud from a national perspective. The ability to work together as members under a national association provides an opportunity to develop tools and shared approaches to combat a major industry problem.

Transportation

Another area in which clearinghouse members have looked to shared approaches is in transportation. Clearinghouse members have the ability to work together to increase the efficiencies of transporting checks from point A to point B. One example of this joint effort regarding transportation is managed by NCHA for members in Texas. Financial institutions typically have similar needs when transporting items from one city to another. The institutions are attempting to deliver the checks at similar deadlines to receive similar availability.

Under this premise in 1995, the former CHAS (now NCHA) developed a joint air transportation program for its membership. Functionally, through an agreement with an awarded vendor, participating members would have door-to-door transportation service for checks processed in Dallas, Houston, and San Antonio for delivery at major cities in Texas. This multilateral approach is managed by NCHA. Additionally, an NCHA committee of participating members provides the forum for both participants and transportation vendors to work together to identify and resolve issues as they develop.

The industry needs in check transportation continue to evolve with the implementations of Check 21 and image exchange solutions. As a result, in 2004, NCHA developed the National Transportation Taskforce, which works with industry partners to manage these changing needs as an industry initiative. In transportation, much of the associated cost is fixed. Whether an airplane transports one check or a million checks, the cost remains much the same. The plane still flies, and the sending bank assumes that cost.

Understanding the industry challenge ahead, the NCHA National Transportation Taskforce looks for ways to create a "soft-landing" approach as those industry needs change for transporting physical paper checks.

Role of the Check Clearing House for the Twenty-First Century

Innovative, dynamic, efficient, adaptable to change—those are the new terms that must be in place for a check clearing-house to be effective in today's world. Gone are the geographic and operational issues that have traditionally been in place and limited financial institutions in their ability to effectively and efficiently exchange paper checks with one another. The check clearinghouse of today must embrace this change and develop initiatives, services, and products to support image sharing and image exchange initiatives.

The method of exchange will continue to evolve, moving ever further into the electronic realm. The need for settlement, however, remains unchanged. Just as in the physical paper check exchange environment, financial institutions have turned to clearing houses as an efficient and effective method for exchange. This need continues and is further enhanced by the migration to electronics.

Additionally, check clearinghouses have the opportunity to play a key role in other related industry initiatives. Whether it is risk management, administering transportation programs, or providing industry training and education, the clearing-house continues to play an important role for the industry. One change for the clearinghouses (similar to the member financial institutions) is that they must be out front in identifying the opportunities that are available and provide those opportunities to membership. The most effective and efficient means for providing new capabilities are through partnerships.

Through partnerships, initiatives, and providing tools for members to effectively manage change, the check clearinghouse is positioned to play a critical role for the industry for many years to come.

Chapter 6

Versatile Check Image Exchange

Jeff Vetterick, Endpoint Exchange LLC

Financial institutions are always looking for new ways to improve the value of and return on their payments franchise. They seek new solutions that draw on the latest technologies to transform payment challenges into opportunities—solutions that enable financial institutions to reduce cost, protect current payment profits, and create new payment revenue streams.

These types of solutions are most valuable when they possess versatility. This includes the ability to work collaboratively, to leverage "relationship capital," and to improvise and improve new solutions within an environment that is heavily invested in multiple technology platforms and existing infrastructure.

Electronic check image exchange has the potential to save the financial services industry billions of dollars. There is a consensus that check image exchange can make a significant impact through reduced operational costs—particularly through the elimination of the costs and inefficiencies associated with the transportation and duplicate processing of paper-based payments. For check image exchange to enjoy an even greater level of growth and adoption, it must provide financial institutions with a new collection of transaction cost advantages that will cause them to change their strategic thinking from the models of the past.

Check image exchange must become more versatile and offer a broad range of capabilities that address the needs of financial institutions of all sizes. We have identified the facets of versatile image exchange. They include:

- Interoperability across standards
- Inter-network operability
- ECCHO Rules compliance
- Large bank/small bank bridge
- Ubiquitous check clearing
- Float optimized image exchange
- Integrated returns and adjustments processing
- National settlement capability
- Low, uniform pricing regardless of Fed District or time of day
- Built-in image quality
- X9.37 support—accepting commingled cash letters
- Energetic thought leadership

Full Interoperability Between All Standard Industry Exchange Formats

The spread of connectivity and check-image-exchange standards is redefining the check-image-exchange channel. National check-image-exchange networks must fully support the X9.37 file format, while also functioning as a translator for disparate, locally used formats between financial institutions. For example, one bank can communicate to the check-image-exchange network in X9.37, while another can communicate in a format uniquely and tightly integrated with their in-house item processing system.

Incorporating new industry standards, such as X9.81, an emerging XML-based standard designed specifically for the exchange of data between banks, will be critical to the continued growth and industry-wide adoption of check image exchange.

Scalability is another critical component to the versatility and success of check image exchange. The national image exchange networks must be equipped to increase capacity as volumes increase. The national image exchange networks should be easily scalable for volumes up to fifty billion items per year.

Full Interoperability Between the National Image Exchange Networks

Viewpointe, headquartered in Charlotte, NC, a leading provider of check-image and Check 21-related services to the nation's top financial institutions, and the Endpoint Exchange Network™, a Metavante company, have established system connectivity for the electronic exchange of check data and images between their respective member financial institutions, with settlement through the National Clearing House Association (NCHA). All members of both Viewpointe and Endpoint Exchange are eligible to take advantage of this increased interoperability. The Viewpointe/ Endpoint Exchange connection will dramatically accelerate the adoption of check truncation and image exchange and enhance the productivity and efficiency of the national check-clearing and settlement system.

The combined reach of Viewpointe and the Endpoint Exchange Network—the imaging technology infrastructure, inte- gration competency, and established customer relationships— will provide an unprecedented level of check image exchange. One of the largest Viewpointe members, Bank of America, was the first in line to implement, sending images from the archive operated by Viewpointe.

By late summer of 2006, the SVPCo Image Payments Network, the electronic-check and check-image-exchange business of The Clearing House Payments Company LLC, and the Endpoint Exchange Network plan to establish full interoperability. The Endpoint/SVPCo connectivity represents another great leap in the growth and interoperability of check image exchange. with the SVPCo Image Payments Network processes an average of 2.3 million items daily, with a daily average dollar value of $6.9 billion, as of this writing.

Connecting the Country's Top-Tier Banks to Mid-Tier and Community Banks

The country's top-tier banks, which clear and settle millions of checks each day, need the ability to exchange with the middle- and low-tier banks for their image exchange programs to reach full potential. Similarly, the ability to exchange electronic items, despite system and platform processing differences and reducing the overhead of managing hundreds of endpoint relationships, provides tremendous value and generates the type of true transaction cost advantage that has been an overriding factor in many top-tier banks joining national image exchange networks and pushing for the interoperability between all the major networks.

The Ability to Clear All Checks Electronically

Until recently this may have seemed like a development that was still a few years down the road, but the technology to clear all checks electronically is here right now.

Check image exchange networks should make available new products designed to provide member institutions with the ability to truncate 100 percent of their forward collection volume. With this type of solution in place, all checks can be accepted, allowing member institutions to clear any check that is otherwise not electronically tradable. When banks enroll in such an option, they enable their organizations to deploy merchant, branch, and other remote capture strategies, while minimizing or eliminating check transportation costs.

These new agency-based settlement programs electronically accept and settle check images drawn on any ABA routing number and handle the downstream item clearing process, while achieving up to 100 percent day-one availability for the collecting institution. The clearinghouse agent institution settles with the sending institution and assumes collection responsibility for those items for all downstream clearing. This includes creating image replacement documents (IRDs) for check images received from the check-image-exchange network and supports the optional electronic clearing of only subsets of checks, such as those with high dollar values.

The check-image-exchange network offering such agency-based programs should first seek to channel items directly and electronically to image exchangeable members or partner, as it normally does, at the lowest possible clearing cost. Only if the item cannot be cleared using this process can it then be routed to the clearing agent to complete the transaction. This type of fully electronic clearing product offers a valuable alternative for the financial institution that is interested in selectively taking advantage of image-based technologies. As those institutions migrate to check image exchange, the networks will automatically route their items through the more cost-effective clearing channel.

Float Optimized Check Image Exchange and Settlement

There is a common belief that, with Check 21, float issues will be neutralized. That may be the case in scenarios with low-dollar check values, or where financial institutions are in close proximity, or where an image exchange agreement is in place, but how can a financial institution achieve float improvement on high-dollar check values when the paying financial institution is across the country and does not accept check images? In that type of scenario, one needs an image exchange platform that works in "near real time" and prioritizes and manages IRDs by high dollar amount for optimum float gain and same-day settlement. Check-image-exchange networks can empower their member financial institutions with tools such as a "High Dollar Analyzer" that determines how much they can improve revenue and collection time by clearing checks faster and with a significant reduction in float.

With near-real-time image exchange, financial institutions would be assured of float improvement with nearly 100 percent same-day or day-one availability of funds. What would this mean for financial institutions? First, there would be more funds available for debt reduction or investing. Second, it would eliminate the need for reserve balances at multiple banks.

Payments make a large contribution to an institution's revenue stream. The country's largest banks generate around 40 percent of their revenue from payments. In today's competitive marketplace, it is in the best interest of financial institutions to deploy a proactive image exchange mechanism that allows float optimization, particularly as interest rates rise.

Efficient Handling of Electronic Returns and Adjustments

National image exchange networks must provide member financial institutions with the capability to electronically return an image of a dishonored check directly to the participating collecting institution as soon as it is identified as non-payable by the institution. This type of real-time decisioning translates into a streamlined returns process. Providing rapidly accelerated return item notification from other institutions on any item forwarded—ideally only minutes later—will ensure better management of loss / risk.

One popular option for the national image exchange networks would include integration with a clearinghouse-provided Internet adjustment feature. Such a feature allows X9.37 interface customers to initiate and respond to adjustments electronically via the Internet, as X9.37 does not provide a standard mechanism for adjustment exchange. Another option would be the support of an advanced adjustments feature that could be directly interfaced with an institution's own adjustments program.

Adjustments are a costly, labor-intensive function for financial institutions. Consequently, the national image exchange networks should eliminate missing/free and listing/recap errors and provide source and target sequence numbers for member institutions at the item level. This would eliminate the need for source-of-receipt requests. The only adjustments generated or responded to would be for traditional encoding errors, duplicate items, or image quality faults.

While it is of great importance to reject duplicate image presentments before they enter the system, financial institutions may occasionally need to adjust back for paper items that are inadvertently sent by the depository bank after the image has been cleared.

The option of adjusting the image rather than paper to accelerate funds reversal and minimize risk will be a necessary component for the continued growth of check image exchange. Redundant adjustments—which sometimes occur in paper-based clearing when depositing, paying, or intermediary processors simultaneously discover the same error—would be dramatically reduced. Preventing redundant adjustments will result in lowered costs, reduced errors, reduced float, and workload optimization.

Partnership with a National Clearing House as National Settlement Agent

Such a settlement agent should provide highly secure, reliable, and cost-effective image and check settlement services to the industry. Agreements between national check-image-exchange networks and a national clearinghouse would bring the major image exchange networks together with the premier settlement provider.

Full Compliance with the Check Image Exchange Rules Established by ECCHO

ECCHO (Electronic Check Clearing House Organization) is recognized and supported as the national provider of clearinghouse rules for electronic check presentment and check image exchange by leading financial services trade associations, clearinghouses, and data processors. These rules facilitate the transition to a more efficient check payment system. Member institutions of national check-image-exchange networks that operate under the ECCHO rules leverage ECCHO membership to ensure that the

collection and settlement of electronic cash letters is controlled
by a common, standard, national rule set. An exchange network's
participating member institutions should automatically be spon-
sored into the ECCHO rule set for all exchanged items, unless the
participant has already secured full ECCHO membership.

Low Uniform Pricing Across Every Federal Reserve District

With check image exchange rapidly growing from a regional to
a national presence, the national check-image-exchange networks
should offer consistent pricing across all twelve Federal Reserve
districts. The ideal check-image-exchange network would provide
standard national pricing regardless of geographic endpoint,
routing number, or time of day (in other words, twenty-four
hours a day, seven days a week). Lower uniform national pricing
would encourage and accelerate the adoption of check image
exchange across the country.

Interface Options that Attract the Country's Leading Check Image Software Developers and Image-Item Processing Outsourcers

The national networks can also do more to promote the
growth and adoption of check image exchange by providing an
application program interface (API) and toolkits to the country's leading check imaging software developers and image-item
processing outsourcers. Check image exchange APIs can and
should provide full interoperability between any item processing
platform, allowing each member institution to exchange images
and data with all other platforms with full transparency.

Utilizing cross-platform architecture, APIs can be designed
to help developers of check and item processing systems tightly
integrate their systems with image exchange network clients—the
node on the network accessed by each participating member's item
processing operation. Such interface options will foster competitive innovation on the part of item-processing-system providers
to continually increase the efficiency of image exchange.

Stringent Check Image Quality Assurance

Providing image-quality-assurance testing on 100 percent of the items passing through a check-image-exchange network should be a free service for every member institution so as to ensure 100 percent member participation, which in turn helps establish more standardization for IQA (image quality assurance) metrics. IQA can run in the background on the exchange network's client gateway (the node on the network installed in each member's check-processing site). The client should handle all traffic into and out of that location and interface with the local item processing system. IQA should test for image quality and usability on each item. IQA should be architected such that it does not interfere with the basic throughput of the network or impede the timeliness of exchange traffic. IQA should be designed to capitalize on the idle resources on the participant's client node, leveraging underutilized CPU resources and distributing the intense IQA load across hundreds to thousands of computers.

As financial institutions forward-present their item images, the IQA software should check each one in real time. Images that are found to have serious and indisputable problems, such as compression or file errors, should be rejected immediately so that they never enter the system. All other items should be carried forward, with the suspect items flagged for the receiving institution's inspection, along with data about which test(s) failed. This will allow the receiving institution to prioritize items that it may wish to review for making an immediate return decision, adjustment decision, or re-scan request.

If the receiving institution wishes, it can return an item on the basis of image quality alone, referencing the appropriate X9.37 return code, well within Reg CC return windows. Member institutions of a check-image-exchange network should have the ability to return items instantly and electronically. Alternatively, receiving institutions should have the discretion to choose to accept a marginal image for presentment purposes. An ideal national check-image-exchange network would provide a built-in re-scan request feature to request a new image from the sender, in accordance with clearinghouse rules. Furthermore, the ability to adjust back poor-quality images discovered outside of the Reg CC return windows should be provided.

The Case for Versatile Image Exchange through the Endpoint Exchange Network

The national payments industry is at a critical phase. A variety of issues from ever-increasing transportation and courier costs to the closing of Federal Reserve check-processing sites have the potential to depress revenues and reduce check payments profit-ability. Moreover, in the past, disparate check imaging platforms isolated financial institutions, creating an environment that discouraged electronic check image exchange.

Image exchange is still in the early phases of its life cycle. Change comes rapidly, and image exchange providers will need to remain nimble and innovative for several years to come.

The rapid growth and success of the Endpoint Exchange Network can be summed up in one word: versatility. The versatility of the Endpoint Exchange Network's approach to interoperability and innovation has eliminated many barriers to entry in image exchange. Through Versatile Image Exchange™, the Endpoint Exchange Network provides all of the aforementioned capabilities to meet the challenges and address the needs of financial institutions of all sizes.

- **Full interoperability between all the image exchange formats**

  Interoperability and scalability are built into Endpoint Exchange. In addition to X9.37, Endpoint Exchange supports emerging XML formats—new standards designed specifically for the exchange of data between banks.

- **Full interoperability between the national check-image-exchange networks**

Endpoint Exchange has established system connectivity for the electronic exchange of check data and images with both Viewpointe and SVPCo, two of the premier national check-image-exchange networks, processing millions of items per day with a multibillion average dollar value.

- **Connecting the country's top-tier banks to mid-tier and community banks**

  Several of the country's largest bank (based on asset size) have joined the Endpoint Exchange Network in order to facilitate image exchange, clearing, and settlement connectivity with mid-tier and community banks. The ability to exchange, clear, and settle electronic items, despite system ad check image platform processing differences, while simultaneously reducing the overhead of managing hundreds of endpoint relationships, provides tremendous value and generates the type of true transaction cost advantage that has been an overriding factor in so many of the country's top-tier banks joining the Endpoint Exchange Network.

- **The ability to clear all checks electronically**

  Endpoint Exchange and M&I Bank offer M&I National Plus, one of the NCHA Image Exchange Plus products designed to provide Endpoint Exchange member institutions with the ability to truncate 100 percent of their forward collection volume. By accepting all checks, M&I Bank is the first Endpoint Exchange Network member to allow other Endpoint Exchange member institutions to clear any check that is otherwise not electronically tradable. M&I National Plus electronically accepts and settles check images drawn on all ABA routing numbers and handles the downstream item clearing process while achieving nearly 95 percent day-one availability for the collecting institution. M&I settles with the sending institution and assumes collection responsibility for those items for all downstream clearing. This includes creating image replacement documents for check images received from the Endpoint Exchange and supports the optional electronic clearing of only checks with high dollar values.

- **Float optimized check image exchange and settlement**

  Endpoint Exchange provides an image exchange platform that works in near real time and prioritizes and manages IRDs by high dollar amount for optimum float gain and same-day settlement. Endpoint Exchange also provides a Web-based "high dollar analyzer" that helps a financial institutions predetermine how much they can improve revenue and collection time by clearing checks faster and with a significant reduction in float through the network. Membership in the Endpoint Exchange Network assures member institutions of float improvement with nearly 100 percent same-day or day-one availability of funds.

- **Efficient handling of returns and adjustments**

  Endpoint Exchange allows financial institutions to electronically return an image of a dishonored check directly to the participating depository institution as soon as it is identified as non-payable by the institution. Real-time decisioning translates into a streamlined returns process. Endpoint Exchange provides rapidly accelerated return item notification from other institutions on any item forwarded—in some cases only minutes later—allowing better management of loss and risk. Endpoint Exchange is tightly integrated with NCHA's Internet adjustments feature, allowing X9.37 interface customers to initiate and respond to adjustments electronically through the NCHA Web site. Endpoint Exchange also supports an advanced adjustments option that can be directly interfaced with an institution's own adjustments program.

- **Partnership with a National Clearinghouse as National Settlement Agent**

  Endpoint Exchange partners with NCHA for national settlement. The NCHA is the nation's largest check-clearing organization providing payment system services to financial institutions of all types and sizes. It operates the nation's first completely automated national settlement system, providing highly secure, reliable, and cost-effective image and check settlement services to the industry. It is the leading settlement provider for the emerging world of check image exchange. The agreement between Endpoint Exchange and NCHA is a significant step for both organizations. It ensures that NCHA will act as the national settlement agent for check image exchange operated by Endpoint Exchange and brings the industry's most versatile check-image-exchange network together with the premier settlement provider.

- **Full compliance with the check-image-exchange rules established by ECCHO**

  The more than four thousand Endpoint Exchange Network member institutions exchange check images under the ECCHO rule set. Endpoint Exchange Network member institutions leverage ECCHO membership to ensure that the collection and settlement of electronic cash letters is controlled by a common, standard national rule set. Every Endpoint Exchange participating member institution not otherwise a full member of ECCHO is covered by the ECCHO rule set for all exchanged items without any additional fees.

- **Low uniform pricing across every Federal Reserve District**

  Endpoint Exchange reduced the interdistrict pricing for all transit check images (before volume-based discounts) effective January 1, 2006. Under this new pricing model, Endpoint Exchange is offering consistent pricing across all twelve Federal Reserve districts. Unlike some check-image-exchange networks, Endpoint Exchange provides low, uniform pricing regardless of the time of day, maintaining its position as the most cost-effective mechanism for national check image exchange.

- **Interface options that attract the country's leading check-image software developers**

  In addition to many of the country's leading financial institutions, the Endpoint Exchange Network membership includes all of the country's leading check imaging software developers and a large number of image-item processing outsourcers. The Endpoint Exchange API (application program interface) is a documented set of protocols by which any item processing system can connect to the Endpoint Exchange network. Utilizing cross-platform architecture, the API is designed to help developers of check and item processing systems make their systems tightly integrate with the Endpoint Exchange Client, the node on the network within each participating member's item processing operation. For participants utilizing the X9.37 interface, Endpoint Exchange provides the client functionality from within its data centers. Endpoint Exchange offers the API at no charge to third-party developers who execute a basic distribution agreement with Endpoint Exchange. The distribution agreement allows the vendor open access to the Endpoint Exchange API documentation, and free ongoing support and development tools, including an online simulator version of the Endpoint Exchange Network exclusively for developer testing. The Endpoint Exchange API provides full interoperability between any item processing platform, allowing each member institution to exchange images and data with all other platforms with full transparency. The API option is ideal for those institutions that wish to take advantage of many of Endpoint Exchange's advanced features, which can only be fully exploited by tight integration with their item processing system. A few of the leading software developers and image-item processing outsourcers that have joined the Endpoint Exchange Network as image exchange distributors and solution developers include Metavante Image Solutions, Jack Henry & Associates, Wausau Financial Systems, and VSoft Corporation.

- **Stringent check-image quality-assurance standards**
  Endpoint Exchange offers image-quality-assurance testing on 100 percent of the items passing through the network as a free service for members. The Endpoint Exchange IQA suite includes over thirty-one tests for image quality and usability, which are performed on each item.

Endpoint Exchange has assumed an active role in forging of new standards, often solving technical and work-process problems that had been unforeseen by the industry as a whole, and in setting industry direction to optimize image exchange for all financial institutions. Endpoint Exchange participates directly in industry workgroups, including the ABA's x9 committee, ECCHO's advisory committee, and NCHA's image committee. Endpoint Exchange also frequently provides thought leadership through speaking engagements at major trade association events.

Endpoint Exchange views check image exchange as an opportunity for financial institutions to gain a competitive edge. Versatile Check Image Exchange™ can help any financial institution reduce costs, protect current payments profits, and "future proof" your payments infrastructure for maximum interoperability.

Metavante Image Solutions provide comprehensive solutions that help banks and businesses transition from paper to electronic payments and image processing. Solutions that can be delivered in-house or outsourced include distributed capture, check and remittance processing, fraud detection, and document and report management. Customers encompass banks and corporations of all sizes worldwide, from de novo banks to the largest financial institutions and corporations. Within Image Solutions, the Endpoint Exchange Network enables U.S. financial institutions to clear their check-based transactions by allowing for the exchange of check images between member institutions. The Endpoint Exchange Network is the country's first electronic check-clearing network that capitalizes on existing imaging infrastructure and settlement relationships, with the interoperability to connect to every endpoint in the nation. Metavante is a registered trademark, and the Endpoint Exchange Network is a trademark of Metavante Corporation.

Chapter 7

Payments System Endgame

David Walker, ECCHO

Introduction

The check died in the 1970s. That is a given. We all wrote it, presented it, and believed it. We must have been right! After more than three decades, in 2006 we are still reading and writing that the check has finally bitten the dust with transaction volume falling and conversions to electronic payments on the rise. The future of payments is ACH, plastic cards, and cell phones.

But wait! The Federal Reserve's *2004 Payment System Study* shows that the check payment system is by far the largest non-cash, non-Fedwire payment system in the U.S. with some thirty-six billion checks cleared each year totaling forty trillion dollars. (See Chart 1.) If the check is no longer an important method of payment, then bank customers must have missed the memo. Many individuals and businesses continue to find value in the check as a payment vehicle as evidenced by their continued usage in very large volumes.

Within the financial industry, however, we seem to be of two minds. One mind is the provocative, sometimes emotional mind that says the check is dead and that we should transition to the endgame as quickly as possible. The other mind is the cautious one that takes measured steps—and then only when it is abundantly clear that many others share the same directional opinion. While some bankers are assuming that check payments will some day cease to exist, the rest of the industry is moving ahead with check image exchange at a pace that is unprecedented for major payment systems.

More than 33 percent of all institutions in the U.S. are already receiving check images totaling almost eight trillion dollars per year and growing very rapidly. Eight trillion dollars is more than three times the total dollar payments made each year via debit and credit cards combined. Everyone will agree that both of these electronic payment methods have been enormously successful.

Let's reconsider the future of the check.

Perhaps It Is Not Yet Dead

In its *2004 Payments System Study*, the Federal Reserve announced a major economic event. Finally, after decades of anticipation, the total number of all electronic payments made in 2003 exceeded the number of check payments. While this is a major milestone in the evolution of payments, there is a propensity to overstate the meaning of this event. Chart 1 shows the distribution of payments volumes and payments dollar amounts across the various payment types.

The chart clearly shows that the check payment system remains, by far, the largest non-cash payment method in the U.S. Comparing payment volumes, the massive check volume is thirty-six billion per year while the second-largest payment method, the credit card, is only nineteen billion. Or, said differently, checks total 189 percent of credit card volume. Comparing payment dollar amounts, the massive check system totals $40 trillion per year while the second-largest payment method, the ACH, is only $25 trillion. This shows that checks are 144 percent of the volume of ACH payments. The check payment system continues to be almost twice as large as the next-largest payment system (excluding Fedwire, which has very large dollars and very small transaction volume).

Chart 1 (source: Federal Reserve's *2004 Payment System Study*)

Payment Type	2003 Volume	2003 Dollars
Checks	36 billion	$40.0 trillion
Credit Card	19 billion	$1.7 trillion
ACH DR & CR	9.1 billion	$25.0 trillion
DR Card	15.6 billion	$.6 trillion
EBT	.8 billion	$.02 trillion

But the volume of checks is declining, so doesn't that suggest that the check is dead and that we just need to accept it and transition rapidly away from the check to other payments? Some pundits suggest that the industry should avoid making any additional investments in a dying payment system and skip directly to the endgame. Before considering the endgame, let's consider the impact of assimilating the volume of check payments into the other payment systems. Both the ACH and the credit card systems are more than thirty years old, and the debit card system is more than twenty years old. After two or three decades of very successful growth, none of these systems are currently processing close to thirty-six billion transactions. How could any, or for that matter, all of them be expected to assimilate the check volume in a very short timeframe? To assimilate that much volume in a short timeframe without major processing disruptions, massive duplications of resources would need to be employed. Not only do these resources already exist in the check system, in the banks, and businesses, but also the existing check resources could not be eliminated as quickly as non-check resources would need to be added. These additional *current period* costs need to be offset by significant *future savings* once all the checks are eliminated. This is not the most positive picture for the shareholders and suggests that checks will be with us and probably in significant volumes for many years.

Let's Go Directly to the Endgame

Each payment type has unique characteristics that make it valuable to the person or organization that selects and uses it. The check, as a payment method, has been around for hundreds of years, and that longevity alone suggests that the check must have one or more enduring qualities. The question as to whether the check should continue to exist is largely one of whether those unique attributes continue to be valuable in today's economic environment. Let's consider that question along with the notion that perhaps we should skip check image exchange and go directly to the endgame.

If we were to describe the payments endgame, it would have all of the following characteristics:

- **Fast** – Transactions should clear expeditiously.
- **Universal payment initiation** – Every participant should be able to initiate the payment as needed to every other participant.
- **Information rich** – Transactions should contain sufficient information to allow customers to immediately identify the transaction as a payment that they initiated without further research or delay.
- **Payment on demand** – The timing of when the payments settle should not be controlled artificially but rather occur as quickly as possible when desired.
- **Abundant legal protections** – Payment participants should be protected by lots of existing legal coverage.
- **Revenue enhancements** – The payment type should support and enhance existing revenue streams.
- **Ubiquitous** – The payment type should enjoy universal acceptance.

- **Use existing capacities and resources** – The payment type should use existing processing capacities rather than duplicating capacities.
- **Product improvements** – The payment type should not obsolete existing customer products and services but rather should enhance them.
- **New value creation** – The payment type should hold the potential for significant new-customer value.

All of these futuristic endgame characteristics describe the current check system. While some are shared by other payment types, no other payment method enjoys all of them. You might question the validity of one of these, so let's focus on that one.

The check is fast? Few individuals would immediately agree that the check is fast because of the physical nature of the paper document and its transportation and processing requirements. Typically, checks are processed multiple times during their life cycles and must be physically transported between the payee, the depositary institution, the paying institution, and any intermediaries. These processes, while performed very efficiently, are time, labor, and capital intensive; thus, the pervasive perspective is that checks are inherently slow. As legal payments, however, checks are inherently fast. Under the law, the check is a demand instrument, and, as such, checks are due and payable on demand. Payees (beneficiaries of payments) can hold on to checks for days, weeks, or even months before deciding to demand payment, or they can present the check to the paying institutions and receive payment *now*.

An example might help. During the 1980s when interest rates reached 21 percent, it was common practice for banks to demand payment immediately on large-dollar checks deposited with them on Fridays. Instead of waiting a day or two for the normal collection processes to deliver the checks to distant (usually eastern) locations, banks would buy airline tickets for their officers, who would hand carry any large-dollar checks to New York, Boston, or Washington, D.C. etc. for direct presentment to the paying bank. The funds would then be sent back using Fedwire to the collecting institution that same day (Friday), thus gaining a two-day (weekend) float advantage. No other payment type allows the depositary institution to achieve this significant expense avoidance for deposited checks. Checks, as demand instruments, have the inherent ability under the law to be very fast. In contrast, if those same large-dollar checks had been converted to any other payment form, settlement of the funds would not have occurred until Monday at the earliest. And in the case of a three-day weekend, settlement would not have occurred until Tuesday at the earliest. Truly, checks are fast.

And there is real value in collecting payments faster. A comparison of two payment scenarios will provide some interesting insight. According to the Federal Reserve's *2004 Payments System Study*, there were $40 trillion in check payments in 2003. Chart 2 includes the following assumptions: (1) that transit checks total $30 trillion, (2) that the interest rate is 5 percent, and (3) that approximately 30 percent of transit checks are cleared the same day they are deposited with 65 percent cleared the next day (leaving 5 percent cleared beyond the first day after deposit). Chart 2 contrasts this typical paper-check-clearing scenario with a best-case ACH clearing scenario and shows the float impact if 100 percent of the transit checks were cleared via the ACH. Because the check is a demand instrument and because ACH transactions are settled no sooner than the day after origination, the loss of float would be approximately $7.5 trillion each year, the value of which is $1 billion per year.

Perhaps the most positive characteristic of ACH payments is that they have predictability of settlement. This is a critical feature of direct deposit of payroll and direct debit services like those for mortgage and insurance payments. As a predictable settlement system, the ACH is ideal for time-sensitive payments when you need assurance that the payment will occur on a particular date. Additionally, the ACH is designed as a float neutral payment system. Under NACHA rules, ACH originations are effective no earlier than the next business day after origination, in part to ensure that all parties have time to receive and process the payments on the same day—thus creating a float neutral transaction. By delaying the effective date for one day, settlement can be accurately predicted.

These unique attributes of the ACH are excellent qualities, but they come at a cost. One major cost is the loss of float. ACH is designed as a float-neutral payment system. Being float neutral is not, however, being "floatless." Check payments are not inhibited by an artificial limitation on how fast transactions can be collected and therefore are well designed to limit, not support, collection delays that create float.

Chart 2 (For illustrative purposes only)

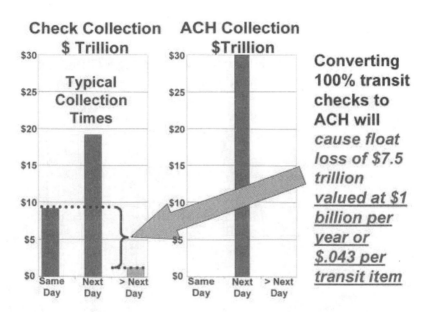

Chart 2 compares an existing paper check system with a non-check electronic payment system. Chart 3 compares an electronic check system (based on image exchange) with the electronic ACH system.

No one knows what percentage of checks might actually be cleared using image exchange once it is fully implemented, but it is safe to say that more checks can be cleared faster using electronics (images) rather than paper checks. Chart 3 assumes that with full implementation only 75 percent of the transit dollars will be cleared the same day, with the remainder cleared the next day.

The potential impact on float is huge with a potential difference of $22.5 trillion per year between the two electronic payment systems. Imagine the financial impact if banks' ACH products had to absorb $3.1 trillion per year in costs. That is the equivalent of thirteen cents for each transaction and is more than the typical ACH revenue. Clearly, this level of assimilation would create major negative impacts to ACH systems including operation, products, and profitability.

Chart 3 (For illustrative purposes only)

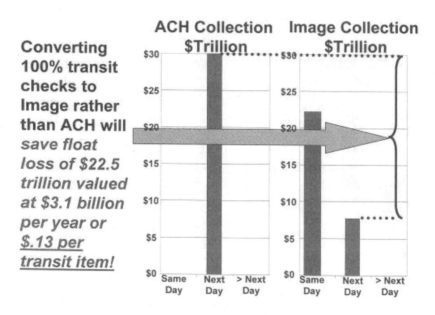

The ACH payment system is an excellent payment system, and these examples are provided not to disparage the ACH but to demonstrate the comparative value of one of the unique characteristics of check payments.

Eliminating Paper from the Check Payment System!

U.S. check law is primarily provided through the Uniform Commercial Code (UCC), but its roots are actually European. The U.S. legal system is a composite of statutory law (passed by legislatures), regulatory law (passed by regulatory authorities) and case law (from litigations and judicial determinations). Aspects of U.S. check law emanate from litigations that actually precede the creation of the U.S., but these litigations did not address the use of technology and electronics in conjunction with check payments. The massive amount of check law has served the check system well across the centuries, but it has also been the primary limitation on the evolution of the check.

During the twentieth century, there was an explosion of technology, and all payment systems experienced rapid and varied enhancements. For checks, those enhancements were limited primarily to the automated processing of pieces of paper with the introduction of magnetic ink character recognition (MICR). The limitations of the law prevented the application of technology to checks in other ways but did not limit the evolution of new electronic-based payment services. While technology was used to create new, high-demand, electronic-based services as lifestyles changed, the check was locked out of evolutionary processes and could not meet the changing needs of its users. Simply put, check law became a significant barrier to progress and artificially redirected creative resources and investments away from checks.

Interestingly, as the volume of the new electronic payments grew, the volume of checks written also continued to grow, thus increasing the overall number of payments. At the bank where this writer was employed in the 1980s, there was a growing number of customer inquiries into the customer service area, which caused a continual increase in staff and expense budget overruns. In an attempt to curb the growth in expenses, it was decided first to price and then subsequently to increase the price of customer service. The volume of customer inquiries continued to grow despite the charges. Finally, an employee observed that the bank was making very good money from this undesirable, labor-intensive, customer-demanded service.

Perhaps, there is a lesson in this that can be applied to checks. During the late twentieth century, bank customers continued to write checks in very large quantities, and so it was increasingly apparent that some other approach was needed to discourage these undesirable, labor-intensive, customer-demanded payments. One approach was to override the customer's decision to make a payment via a check by converting the check in the middle of the collection process to a non-check. This approach created customer service problems, devalued bank product offerings, and caused a significant loss of bank revenue without offsetting reductions in bank costs. Another approach, Check 21, supported the customer's payment decision to use a check and also encouraged the transition to a much more efficient check system.

Check 21 Act

The Check 21 Act was designed to encourage banks to stop the transportation and processing of the original paper checks early in the check collection and return processes. Prior to Check 21, banks (all depositary financial institutions including commercial banks, savings banks, banker's banks, credit unions, etc.) that wished to truncate the original check had to get the agreement of all the parties with an interest in the check. Achieving universal acceptance of check truncation would have required the agreements of more than sixteen thousand institutions and tens of millions of bank customers. Check 21 addressed this barrier to check electronification head-on by providing that agreements are not needed among the parties so long as the original check is replaced with another, newly defined, paper payment document entitled a "substitute check."

Check 21 does not require that all institutions accept checks in the form of electronic transactions, but it does eliminate the primary legal obstacle to check truncation—the need for all those agreements. No longer does any truncating institution need to fear that its customers would be wooed away by a competitor promising the return of their original checks, and no longer can any bank customer demand that it receive its paid original paper checks back in its statements. Check 21 dramatically changed industry and customer expectations and opened the door to check truncation, which in turn encourages the use of technology to significantly enhance the check payment system. The *check* payment system ceased to be the *paper check* system. The U.S. Congress, reacting to a proposal from the Federal Reserve, initiated a dramatic change and began the transition of the medium (paper) rather than the instrument (the check) and provided a new option for clearing checks.

Check 21 Does Not Validate Check Image Exchange

The new law does not validate check image exchange. Check 21 authorizes the unilateral truncation of a paper check only when it is replaced with a substitute check, but it does not validate the exchange of check payments electronically. Check image exchange must be preceded by agreements between the parties to accept the images, and no institution can be forced to accept check images. The downside of exchanging in the absence of an agreement would be smaller if the risks were small, but to exchange check images outside of an agreement is to do so without the support of the statutory, regulatory, or case law and includes an indeterminately large amount of risk. Since the law does not cover electronic check exchange, it is unclear to whom the courts might assign liability and in what amounts whenever disputes arise. In paper check law, there is the potential for "proximately caused damages," or consequential damages. Should the courts determine that the award of consequential damages is appropriate, there is no statutory or regulatory guidance to assist the courts in making a fair determination as to how much and to which parties awards should be made. This raises the level of uncertainty as to the outcome of litigations and also the expense of litigations. The solution to mitigate this risk is to have agreements between the exchanging parties.

There are several agreement options from which banks might choose. These range from two-party agreements that bind only the two parties, multiparty agreements such as through a provider of image services, or clearinghouse agreements. In two-party agreements and multiparty agreements, only those agreeing are bound. Both of these approaches could be better than exchanging without any protections, but the preferred option is to have legal coverage through clearinghouse rules. Clearinghouses have two unique characteristics under the UCC. They can vary or clarify certain aspects of the law, and when transactions are exchanged under clearinghouse rules, all parties with an interest in the transactions are covered by the rules even if they are unaware of the clearinghouse or its rules. Of course, clearinghouses do not have unlimited ability to vary the law, but these two aspects equip clearinghouses with the ability to provide broader coverage and therefore protections than institutions could obtain under two-party or multiparty agreements. In the U.S., the Electronic Check Clearing House Organization (ECCHO) is the only clearinghouse with a comprehensive set of image exchange rules. ECCHO enjoys board acceptance across the industry. Additional information on clearinghouse rules is available at www.eccho.org.

It's Moving Too Slowly

Major changes in payments systems in the U.S. tend to evolve over an extended period of time. Recent "overnight" success stories in ACH and debit card payments reflect rapid growth in very recent periods, but both of these payment types have existed for more than twenty years. During most of their histories, they exhibited slow growth. Even with their rapid growth in recent years, the volume of debit card and card transactions are still small relative to check volumes.

Chart 4 (Chart source: Federal Reserve/ECCHO Communications Work
Group Data sources: Federal Reserve, NCHA, and SVPCO)

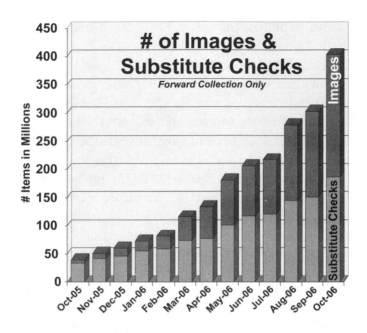

In light of the historically slow progress of change in the
payments systems, the rate of implementation of Check 21 and
check image exchange is phenomenally fast. Chart 4 shows the
volume trend by month from October 2005 through October
2006. During the short thirteen month period shown in the
chart, the volume has grown from only 39.4 million checks per
month to 403.0 million per month. The October 2006 volume
annualized totals 4.6 billion checks per year. Additionally, Chart
4 shows that the earliest volume growth was in substitute checks.
This should not be a surprise.

The use of Check 21 and substitute checks provides a bridge
between paper exchange and image exchange. Each bank is
ready to send and receive images at different times based on
each institution's priorities and available resources. Substitute
checks, under Check 21, provide a means for two banks to enjoy

the benefits of a more efficient collection system without having to wait until every bank is ready to both send and receive. The bridge step between the traditional paper collection process and a new image collection is a hybrid approach that uses image on one end and paper on the other. Once both institutions have implemented image exchange, the interim bridge using substitute checks can be eliminated.

The number of substitute checks is, therefore, an early indicator of future image volume. By October 2006, the distribution of volume between images and substitute checks was 53.8 percent image and 46.2 percent substitute check.

Chart 5 (Chart source: Federal Reserve/ECCHO Communications Work Group Data sources: Federal Reserve, NCHA, and SVPCO)

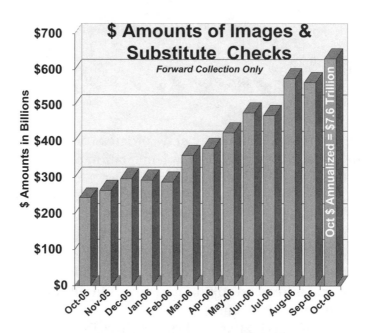

Chart 5 shows the dollar amount of the checks that has been replaced with either substitute checks or images. The annualized October 2006 dollar amount totals $7.6 trillion per year. That is an amazing amount of money and is more than the combined total of all debit card and credit card payments. According the Federal Reserve's 2004 Payment System Study, the dollar amount of all debit card payments during 2003 was $.6 trillion, and credit card payments totaled $1.7 trillion. Combined, these two payment types total only about 30 percent of the dollars cleared via substitute check and check image, and that is only twenty-four months after the effective date of Check 21.

Chart 6 shows the number of routing transit number (R/T) receiving check images by month through October 2006. As of October 2006, about 6,000 R/Ts were receiving check images. These equal approximately 33% of the total number of U.S. institutions.

Chart 6 (Chart source: Federal Reserve/ECCHO
Communications Work Group

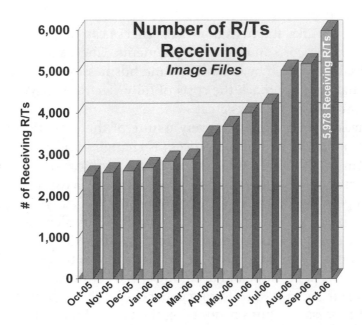

Summary

Checks are the largest non-cash, non-Fedwire payment system in the U.S. This is true whether measured in terms of the volume of payments or in terms of the dollar value of the payments. This massive system still includes tens of billions of checks and tens of trillions of dollars each year in payments.

Checks will continue to contribute significant value to financial institutions and their customers because checks have a unique combination of characteristics that does not exist in any other payment type. No other single payment system can replace 100 percent of the check payments without major cost duplications and virtual recreations. These characteristics along with the universal acceptance of checks and the existing capital investments in the check-processing infrastructure ensure that check payments will continue be a critical part of the payments system for many years to come.

By applying technology to checks, significant costs can be eliminated or reduced. As these costs decline and the infrastructure shrinks, the costs to process checks can be expected to approach the costs of electronic payments. Checks are almost universally accepted by individuals and businesses alike, and as costs match or approach the costs of fully electronic payments, the future of checks looks great.

Check 21 is changing the very nature of the collection and return of checks and in the process is changing the associated economics. By eliminating the need for physical transportation between institutions and by facilitating electronic image exchange, Check 21 is finally accomplishing the early elimination of paper processing. The acceptance and implementation of these changes are further accelerated by the Federal Reserve's decisions to eliminate many of its processing sites across the U.S. The Fed's decision and declining check volumes overall are pushing up the cost of collecting paper checks through the traditional processes—thus encouraging the use of image exchange as the preferred collection method.

As of the end of October 2006, only twenty-four months after the effective date of Check 21, significant progress has been made in the transition from paper to electronics. Already, more than 33 percent of all the institutions in the U.S. are receiving images. Additionally, when annualized, the dollar amounts of substitute checks and check images exchanged total $7.6 trillion dollars. This is more than three times as much as the total dollar amounts for all debit card and credit card payments combined. This transition to check image exchange is progressing at a record pace, much faster than any other major payments transition in U.S. history.

It is clear that the industry is aggressively embracing a better check system—one that is image based. The pioneers are already well out in front. When institutions delay implementing check image exchanges, they risk diminished competitive ability, increased collection and return costs, diminished customer values, and lowered earning for their shareholders. The time for enhancing your institution's check services is now. The endgame includes all payment systems with their unique characteristics, and it also includes checks. Transition the medium not the instrument.

Chapter 8

Complex Payments

Robert F. Kirk, Vicor, A Metavante Company

Financial institutions and businesses are faced with a complex world when it comes to managing payments. To thrive, each entity must manage a multitude of variables ... as we will operate in a blended world for the foreseeable future.

Overview

More than ever before, financial institutions and their corporate customers are faced with a changing and complex world when it comes to payment processing. Each entity must manage a multitude of payments variables on a transaction-by-transaction basis. Each payment process has its own rules, standards, regulatory requirements, and risk. Each banking relationship may require proprietary formats and processes and security protocols. Each supplier may require a unique interface to its systems. And for the foreseeable future, financial institutions and their corporate customers must efficiently process both electronic and paper-based payment streams, each requiring, at a minimum, its own processes, rules, and reporting requirements. Clearly, the payment processing landscape is a complex environment.

Managing these complex payments means tying together disparate systems, which means some form of enterprise integration. And so companies have set out to integrate payments information with all due haste; they write custom interfaces between systems, rekey data, dedicate specialists to resolve payment exceptions, maintain spreadsheets, and try to get the job done. Unfortunately, cobbling payments systems together isn't enough.

The question for financial institutions and their corporate customers to ask is: "When will the complex payments world become less fragmented and easier to migrate?" That answer is: "Unfortunately, not in the foreseeable future!"

The right question now is: "What payment systems, architectures, and processes are required to help run the business in this complex environment, save time and money, attract new customers, generate new revenue, and leverage existing technology investments?" The answer to that question is fairly simple. Systems are needed that can efficiently and economically manage the blended world of paper and electronics while ensuring flexibility for internal business processes along with consolidation of critical payment data for cash management.

This chapter outlines four major topics:
1. Complex payments
2. Market examples where complex payment processing is required
3. Solution architecture
4. Corporate Payment Progress Index, an industry index that measures the progress of corporate payments

Complex Payments

Succinctly stated, complex payments are defined as those that are content rich and require the management of a multitude of variables on a transaction-by-transaction basis. Complex payment processing is required in many major industries and multiple market segments. Simple payments, on the other hand, are exactly what their name implies. They are primarily cash and low-value electronic consumer-card transactions with little or no payment instructions or associated information. Largely for this reason, the market for simple payments is applicable to the consumer segment. Since the channel for simple payments is electronic (excluding cash)—with well-defined processes and well-established standards—and the payee sets rules, there also are few payments exceptions.

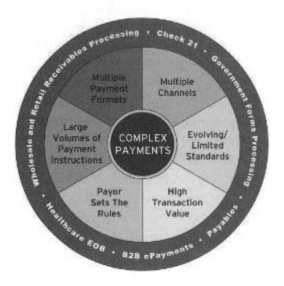

Complex payments, on the other hand, are quite different. How? In six critical ways:

1. Multiple payment formats

Complex payments may arrive or depart in paper (check, money order, or traveler's check), electronic (wire transfer, electronic data interchange, automated clearinghouse) or card-based (purchase card) format. Each format requires a unique workflow process, security, and financial network for clearing and settlement.

2. High average transaction value

Complex payments have an average transaction value of greater than $3,000 versus an average of $115 for a simple transaction, according to the *Nilson Report*. Higher transaction values require more attention for authorization and overall quality inspections.

3. Large volumes of instructions and related information

Complex payments include large volumes of instructions and related information, typically in multiple formats and data structures. Complex payments, for example, average four pages of payment instructions per transaction, usually with multiple line items on each page; no wonder that 96 percent of invoices processed for payments require keying of data from paper—a costly, time-consuming, and error-prone task. Additionally, the development of standards for the transmission of remittance data is the one industry initiative that lacks any momentum—a major barrier for conversion to electronic-based commercial payments as discussed below.

4. Multiple channels for receivables and payables

Complex payments have multiple channels for receiving and disbursing payments—from mail, Internet, and phone to branch capture and accounting packages—each with their own level of unpredictability in volume and frequency, as well as unique processing and security requirements.

5. Lack of standards

There are limited standards for complex payments—and none on the invoice processing and ERP posting side. As one example, no single standard exists for remittance information—a barrier to improving the efficiency of the financial supply chain cited by 79 percent of respondents to a survey by the Association for Financial Professionals (AFP). As another example, accounting systems typically are not integrated with electronic payments systems; 64 percent of respondents to the AFP survey singled this out as a barrier to improving financial supply chain efficiency. And standards are not well-defined for business-to-business (B2B) electronic invoice presentment and payment (EIPP).

This hampers not only the adoption of the technology but also the potential operational efficiencies provided by this service. Contrast this lack of standards with simple payments, where message formats, security protocols, and overall operating rules are well defined by the card associations, VISA and MasterCard.

6. Payers set the "rules"

With complex payments, "rules" are set by the payer. This means, for instance, that one payment may be consolidated for multiple invoices by the payer, leading to a high percentage of exceptions and manual intervention by the processing financial institution.

Considering these characteristics of complex payments—along with the results from a recent survey among a hundred global banks that shows 84 percent are generally satisfied with their current approach to payments processing (Economist Intelligence Unit 2005)—we should not expect revolutionary changes anytime soon to this complex environment.

Market Segments

While simple payments, by definition, are limited largely to consumer applications, complex payments impact a much broader range of market segments, including but not limited to:

- Wholesale banking—payables and receivables
- Healthcare
- Government forms processing
- Mortgage
- Insurance
- Brokerage
- Others

Each segment (and each company within a segment) has specific requirements, businesses processes, and product offerings that dictate unique processing methods for payment management.

Receivables

With only 20 to 25 percent of B2B payments processed through a wholesale lockbox in the United States, and corporate clients of the financial institution demanding more receivables information, banks are expanding their receivables services to strengthen existing client relationships, attract new customers, enter lucrative markets, and drill deeper into their existing markets.

Complex payments automation drives this trend by enabling greater integration between receivables and lockbox systems for tracking and managing the financial supply chain. And Check 21 assists further by accelerating postings and enabling distributed capture and digital clearing. Among the receivables services now being offered by banks are:

- Automated capture of receivables and customer information such as invoice data, demographic information on remittance coupons, or requests for more information
- Consolidation of paper-based and electronic payment streams, regardless of whether the lockbox provider was the original recipient of the electronic payment
- Use of color scanning for the delivery of check and document images that more closely replicate original, paper-based receivables and make images more usable
- Integration with accounting applications for automated receivables matching
- Remote check capture for accelerating the processing and/or electronic conversion of payments received outside of a lockbox or the normal receivables process
- Customized business rules for handling industry-specific receivables such as the processing of explanation of benefits (EOB) in the healthcare profession
- Deposit reconcilement for tracking deposits from multiple departments

- Electronic bill presentment and payment (e-bills)
- Order processing
- Collections

Companies using outsourced receivables services—regardless of the function—often eliminate so-called "information float," the delay in accessing receivables data. Outsourced receivables services also rein in substantial costs associated with reconciling complex transactions where invoice processing costs alone have risen 37 percent in the past four years, according to the Institute of Management and Administration. And outsourced receivables services can assist the financial institutions' corporate clients in the timely resolution of payments exceptions, which cost the U.S. economy seven hundred billion dollars a year, according to the Commerce Department.

Through the heavy lifting of complex payments automation, companies can receive real-time information from invoices that can be integrated into their ERP and CRM systems or fed into industry-specific solutions that apply logic to how receivables should be handled. A good example is explanation of benefits (EOBs) statements in the medical insurance arena. And once receivables data has been captured and archived, companies can use it to learn more about their customers to improve cash forecasting or negotiate better contract terms.

Companies that outsource their receivables also point to less-quantifiable benefits, such as senior management spending less time chasing payments exceptions. A/R exceptions have a negative effect on nearly every department of a corporation, including treasury, sales, recordkeeping, customer service, shipping, and manufacturing. With resolutions taking up to 120 days, these exceptions can adversely affect operations, suppliers, inventory turns, trade credit, borrowing costs, and day sales outstanding (DSO). The data capture provided by the complex payments solutions offered by banks can help speed the resolution of exceptions and plug the resource drain they cause.

But the biggest benefit for billers may be the increased control and visibility that these receivables services provide. Once a corporate biller has its receivables data, it can do data mining, drill down into the information, access more meaningful reports, and electronically monitor what's going on with its financial supply chain—even with its partners and clients. Users across the corporate financial supply chain—sales, manufacturing, shipping, treasury, collections, etc.—can far more easily access information for proactively addressing payments disputes and discrepancies and even preventing payments issues from occurring.

None of these receivables functions would be possible without complex payment automation.

Payables

Many banks' trade services departments have identified a need for delivering international trade payables management and financing for large corporate customers. Offering payables services to their clients would give banks two distinct sources of revenue: transaction fees from the management of the payables function and income from financing customer purchases. For banks targeting the payables space, complex payments solutions provide an automated platform from which they can service their clients.

Trade payables management presents a unique paper-to-electronic process requiring defined business rules and routing of images and data. The typical trade payables workflow includes invoice identification; data and invoice verification; business rules matching and routing; and data delivery via flat files, XML, or direct interface to ERP systems. Solutions for automating the process must support both electronic data and paper documents. In cases where the buyer sends paper documents, the bank must use the latest imaging technology and capture key data. In cases where the buyer sends electronic data, the bank requires a direct interface to the buyer's ERP system.

Moreover, input for trade payables management solutions requires support for electronic data entry by buyer and seller, paper document inputs, facsimile data capture, and direct capture from e-mail—hardly the sort of inputs supported by traditional receivables processing systems. Thankfully, solutions for optimizing complex payments meet these requirements.

Healthcare

Healthcare payments processing is tailor-made for complex payments processing. These solutions can automate data capture and the reconciliation of billing discrepancies between providers and payers. Today, differences between contracted services and the services provided to patients results in a large amount of manual data entry and exceptions processing. The delays caused by exceptions resolution, in turn, result in longer DSO for the provider.

Seeing a business opportunity, financial institutions increasingly are looking at becoming adjudicators of these discrepancies, resolving differences quickly using online workflow automation and user-configurable business rules to identify and correct exceptions.

That's where complex payments automation comes in. These solutions combine workflow automation, advanced data capture, and rules-based decisioning engines to deliver a business process management platform suited to the complex rules and processes of a healthcare payments environment. This type of complex payments platform works in conjunction with the financial institution's current receivables processing system, providing the processes necessary to facilitate the adjudication and rebilling of denied claims to the provider. The platform does this by comparing the EOB or 835 reject code to the current contract terms and rebilling.

Another opportunity for complex payments solutions in healthcare is the handling of denied claims, which represent the highest state of financial exposure for provider organizations. Using complex payments technology, processors can access denied claims management reports, which can help providers manage denials and unearth recoverable revenue. By integrating

Check 21 technology and processes, providers can further improve cash flow.

Together, these opportunities highlight the exceptional value of complex payments solutions.

Government Forms Processing

There are few applications better suited to complex payments processing than specialized government forms processing. Dealing with government services processing means dealing with very particular, very demanding requirements that present potential risks for the end user.

In general, specialized government services require highly adaptive, highly secure platforms to automate the processing of very complex forms with a tremendous degree of accuracy. These systems must have strong capabilities for both machine and hand-print recognition. They often have to manage the relationship among fields on individual forms, as well as fields on a variety of supplemental forms that may or may not be present. And they have to perform these data requirements quickly in order to meet tight turnaround times. In addition, the systems must meet the government's notoriously high security standards.

Despite daunting requirements, complex payments technology can deliver remarkable benefits for specialty government applications. Through sophisticated forms processing and character recognition technologies, users can improve the quality of data captured and reduce manual keying—which are critical to meeting tight processing windows and keeping labor costs under control. Errors are eliminated through system databases and complex business rules, ensuring various processing situations are handled correctly.

And complex payments solutions can support the electronic clearing of all checks—an emerging requirement for government users as they look to take advantage of Check 21—which will help government agencies accelerate posting to get faster access to much-needed funds.

A Complex Environment

If we must operate and manage payment processing in this complex environment, how do we ensure cost control, profitability, and innovation? We need a solution platform that can optimize complex payment processing for multiple payment formats and in multiple market segments. For instance, in a receivables environment where there is a mix of incoming paper and electronic transactions with large volumes of invoice data, complex payments optimization delivers cost savings by employing highly effective workflows, consolidated reporting, and data exchange across multiple payment formats.

In a cash management or treasury services environment, complex payments optimization can help streamline related processes, including high-value, bulk, and cross-border transactions.

Meantime, in a distributed capture environment where a corporation electronically manages paper checks and invoices and transmits them to its bank for deposit, complex payments optimization provides the depositor with accelerated funds availability and operational savings, while its bank reaps enhanced efficiencies and new revenue opportunities.

Similarly, for Check 21-enabled banks, complex payments optimization drives real-time image analysis, enabling fraud safeguards as well as risk management for image exchange.

Solution Architecture

The strategy for optimizing complex payments consists of incorporating tools for eliminating duplicative efforts, minimizing manual processes, and centralizing administration and operations for an enterprise of payment systems. Further, the solution has to provide connectivity to move payments and data between channels, systems, and applications no matter the format (paper, electronic, or card-based), standards, rules, or processes they use. To get there from here, financial institutions and businesses can turn to new solutions for optimizing complex payments that can handle:

- **Paper and electronic formats**
  There's an old saying that payment mechanisms are never eliminated, only added. Case in point is the paper check. Despite all the hype about a checkless society, between sixty and seventy percent of commercial payments are currently made via paper check, according to the *Nilson Report*. Even with the recent enactment of Check 21, industry analysts project that commercial check volumes will still total eleven billion in 2020, with the dollar value of those checks actually rising. In light of the staying power of checks, any complex payments solution must be able to seamlessly handle both paper and electronic transactions.

Commercial Check Volume

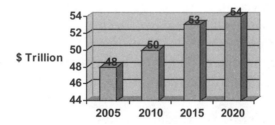

Commercial Check - Transactions

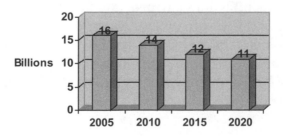

- **Complex workflows**

  Solutions will require sophisticated workflow tools to bridge the disparate formats, processes, and rules used in complex payments to seamlessly automate all payments and to consolidate data into a single view for critical cash flow reporting and visibility. The proliferations of new payment channels—wireless, mobile, telephone, and online—will only add complexity to the payments environment.

- **ERP Integration**

  Complex payments optimization solves the rigid connectivity issues with ERP systems, enabling electronic updates and integration into SAP, Oracle, and such.

- **Broad reporting requirements**

  Complex payments optimization facilitates comprehensive reporting for bank customers and in multiple formats including paper, electronic, and physical storage mediums. Financial institutions continue to see greater demand from their corporate clients for timely access to consolidated payment information.

- **Visibility across the enterprise on payments information**

  Complex payments optimization consolidates all transaction information across the enterprise, providing the visibility into payments that is critical to complying with regulatory mandates. Moreover, achieving an enterprise view of payments may be necessary to ensuring future payment profitability according to a majority of the banks, intermediaries, and networks polled by the Global Concepts research firm.

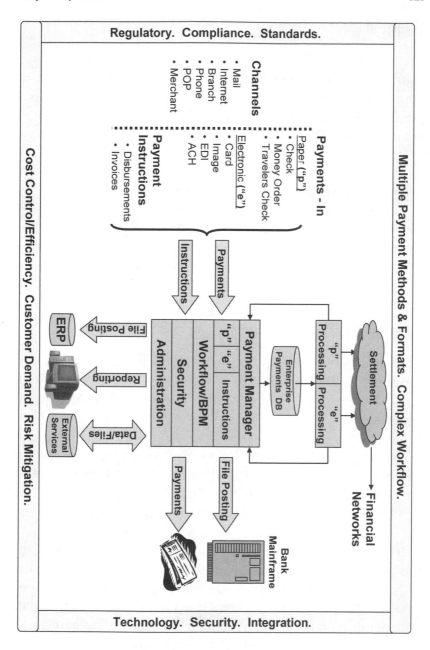

The Payoff

Is dramatically minimizing the multitude of variables associated with payment processing an industry dream? Not on your life. Optimizing the management of complex payments is possible, and multiple benefits across the financial supply chain are numerous. They include:

- Greater visibility of payment transactions
- Increased operational efficiency
- Superior business processes
- Maximized cash reserves investments
- Compliance with regulatory changes
- Improved operational risk management
- Increased customer retention

Corporate Payment Progress Index

How do we know if the corporate payment industry is making progress? And if it is making progress, how much and at what rate? What is driving the progress, and what is restricting the progress?

To help measure the progress and direction of corporate payments, VICOR has developed and established the Corporate Payment Progress Index (CPPI). Succinctly stated, the VICOR CPPI quantifies the progress of corporate payments.

The objective in developing the VICOR CPPI is to help the industry at-large to truly understand and quantify the broad situation of corporate payments and the projected direction from the perspective of corporate payment executives. A great deal of data and quantitative information exists within the payments industry for all major categories (consumer and business payments, etc.). A majority of this information results from comprehensive research from highly credible sources. However, a consolidated view of corporate payments is not available. The specific objectives consist of the following:

- Understand the corporate payment market at a level that considers all payment types
- Obtain detailed information about needs and requirements to support product and market development plans

Multiple stakeholders within the payments industry will benefit from the CPPI. Corporate payment managers will obtain a broad perspective on the payments function and understand how their situations and associated plans compare to their peers. Financial Institutions will obtain a consolidated understanding and a different perspective on the payments industry—a large source of their revenue and profitability—and better understand the needs and plans of their customers and prospects. Technology and solution providers will have access to information that will help focus their product development and deployment plans.

The VICOR CPPI is based upon a scale of 0 to 100 and is divided into three major zones:

1. **Room for improvement** (0–35), which is characterized by low satisfaction, high cost, and low investment in high-share payment methods

2. **Moderate progress** (36–65), which is characterized by general satisfaction, costs under control, and even investment distribution

3. **Strong progress** (66–100), which is characterized by high satisfaction, low cost, and high investment in high-share payment methods.

The VICOR CPPI uses the share of the various payment methods, on a weighted-average basis, as the foundation for determining three subindices:

- Cost/transaction index
- Investment index
- Satisfaction index

Each of the three subindices is based upon a scale of 0 to 100, with movement toward 100 being a positive trend. The sum of the three subindices, when equally weighted, determines the VICOR CPPI.

Summary

Clearly, we operate in a complex world when it comes to payment processing, and the situation is not going to change anytime soon. Payment processing will require the management of multiple variables for a long time to come. Financial institutions and businesses must accept this situation as an opportunity, not a problem. Solutions are available today to help manage this complex world—solutions that deliver the innovation required to stay ahead in a highly competitive complex payment environment.

Chapter 9

The Commercialization of the ACH: How CheckFree Became a Leader

Mark A. Johnson, CheckFree Corporation

CheckFree has, over a thirty-year period, become the leading provider of ACH software and processing services in the United States. By 2006, the company was serving twenty million consumers, fifteen thousand financial institutions, and three thousand corporations. How CheckFree achieved this leadership position is a story of vision, risk taking, and perseverance. What follows is that story.

In 1975, I began working for the Federal Reserve Regional Check Processing Center (RCPC) in Columbus, Ohio. The Federal Reserve was dedicated to replacing checks with a more efficient process and was launching the Automated Clearing House (ACH) to become a credible, alternative payment channel. By 1975, the Federal Reserve was quickly rolling out ACH operations across the country at each of its regional offices. As a management trainee, I was assigned to work in the new ACH department at the Fed.

At the time, however, the ACH really wasn't the Automated Clearing House, but was more like the "somewhat" Automated Clearing House. Since the Federal Reserve offices were not yet connected electronically to transmit ACH transactions, tapes were mailed. Our first government application was with the Air Force in regards to its retirement payments. At the Columbus office, we received a tape that was mailed every month from the Air Force in Denver containing the Air Force retirement transactions. When we processed the file for "electronic" receiving banks, we created tapes with their transactions. For non-electronic banks, almost all of the banks, we created a paper listing to be sent to them by the Federal Reserve's check courier system. To process a tape, we were required to create a control document by typing an eighty-character record on a key punch card.

At the time, the legal framework was still being developed by regional automated clearinghouse organizations. Each region formed an automated clearinghouse association, a nonprofit organization made up of member institutions that agreed upon a set of bylaws and rules for exchanging commercial items. The regional associations formed the National Automated Clearing House Association, which became known as NACHA. It was an association of associations to agree nationally on rules. This then allowed the banks to have a legal framework among them to exchange items.

During my first twelve months at the Federal Reserve, we began to add a number of additional originators. First, we added Air Force active pay and then Social Security SSI payments, followed by SSA payments. We also processed our first commercial application—life-insurance premiums that were deducted automatically from accounts. By 1978, ACH systems were linked electronically nationwide, thanks to NACHA and the Federal Reserve Bank. This created a standard, low-cost, high-volume payment system for domestic transactions nationwide.

The government soon gave the system even more credibility by initiating efforts to promote it to Social Security beneficiaries and other government-benefits recipients. This placed ACH on the map and began the push for more banks to invest in systems to process these new transactions. Demand blossomed seemingly overnight, and Stockholders Systems (SSI) became one of two companies to market an ACH processing system to banks across the country during that time. One of the two companies that became technology providers serving the ACH was well on its way.

CheckFree

During this time, Pete Kight, the founder of CheckFree, was managing some Nautilus clubs in Houston, Texas. He was a college athlete who was sidelined by an injury. But sports and the spirit of competition were in his blood. Managing health clubs first got him thinking about the commercialization of the ACH. At the time, clubs were selling annual memberships that were purchased once a year, and decisions were sometimes made in a hard-sell situation. The industry's primary challenge was that when the anniversary date arrived a significant number of members didn't renew. Pete recognized that a monthly payment system where the membership renewed automatically would significantly reduce the membership churn. In addition, it would allow the clubs to even their cash flow over the course of the year. This allowed the staff to spend more time servicing the customers rather than selling memberships.

Pete wanted to utilize an approach that allowed him to collect monthly fees without mailing bills and waiting on a check to be sent. An insurance executive suggested that he look into a paper draft system, which the insurance industry had used successfully. A banker suggested he use the ACH system, which would be less costly to implement. He tested a basic system at his clubs, and even with all the challenges of the early ACH at that time, the system worked. More important, the health clubs were profitable much earlier in the month with this new business model. Pete immediately saw this approach as a nugget of a great business idea. At the time, he was nearly broke, but with $777.00 in savings to start the business, he moved back home to Columbus,

Ohio. There he started Aegis Systems in the basement of his grandmother's house in 1981.

Pete needed to find customers and potential partners to help him get his business off the ground. He thought this was the kind of service that a bank should want to offer. His dad had a long-time relationship with City National Bank, which changed its name a few years later to Bank One, so he approached the bank. Bankers are notoriously buttoned-down and conservative; however, City National was considered an innovative bank, particularly around electronic payments. Although he was able to get a meeting, he didn't get much interest from the senior executives. They viewed Aegis as a small company with a lot of work ahead before it could become a business worthy of a bank the size of City National. They were glad to gain his business as a customer, but they shuffled him off to the operational staff.

Pete was able to sign his first customers, who were apartment owners, in his new service, which he called "CheckFree." To prove the concept, Pete went door to door to sign up renters to pay rent automatically. Through the process, he learned how to position the service. Phrases such as "debiting your account" were consumer unfriendly. Nobody wanted to sign up if you offered that. However, you didn't get much resistance if you told a consumer, "We'll have your bank pay it for you."

I had left the Federal Reserve in 1978 to join City National Bank. After a short period there, I was given responsibility for cash management operations, which included implementing and servicing ACH customers. I was asked to work with Pete to implement Aegis as a customer. After Pete signed a large racquetball chain, he asked me to consider joining him at CheckFree. At the time, I was married but didn't have children yet. It was a risk, and I knew the amount of time that would be involved. But I agreed to join him in 1982. My wife was a schoolteacher and worked with us during the first summer. She joked that it was the only time she got to see me.

By then, Pete had moved the business out of his grandmother's basement into a house that he shared with a family business. Our office expanded from that house to the house next door. We literally operated out of two houses, with cables running between them. We didn't do much for property values, and I'm sure we broke some building codes. We also decided to drop the Aegis name and rename the company "CheckFree."

Health Clubs

Pete then came across the owner of a health club who wanted to use the service, which had been Pete's idea all along. By now, it was the early 1980s, and the club industry was starting to grow by leaps and bounds but still had large membership-churn issues. In 1982, the majority of clubs were very sales driven. They wanted to sign up as many members as possible. What they often did to drive up business was offer very low annual fees. They then hoped that no one showed up, frankly, because they weren't necessarily equipped to handle the volume. It was a risky and stressful way to operate. Nevertheless, their projections were usually correct. Most people did not show up on a regular basis.

Some progressive club owners decided that they wanted to change this by going to monthly membership fees, but they didn't have a cost-effective way of doing so. CheckFree's solution filled that void. The solution has been attributed with transforming the industry by providing a recurring-revenue business model. Clubs that had constantly operated in survival mode began to thrive. Fluffy white towels began showing up in locker rooms. Juice bars with bottled water retailing for two dollars and juice retailing for three dollars became the norm. Exercise classes expanded their offerings. Owners realized they could transform their clubs into service-based operations and make a lot more money. Clubs quickly became a place where people wanted to relax and unwind.

This changed the dynamic of the industry. The entire industry began adopting the ACH-based solution, and CheckFree was at the forefront, signing up close to a hundred accounts in the next twelve months.

To keep up with the growth, we hired a lot of young, aggressive individuals. In the 1980s, our business culture was casual, energetic, and focused—very much the image that people now associate with high-tech start-ups of the 1990s. We had beer blasts, chili parties, barbecues, and lots of late-night pizza. Even though it was a very exciting time, there was also a lot of stress— stress in signing up customers, stress to deliver what we sold, stress to solve problems, and stress to pay the bills. We had a lot of churn and burn with our associates. Many people simply were not prepared for the long hours and fast-paced, high-pressure work environment.

In addition to health clubs, we began to call on larger corporations. For corporations to implement an ACH debit service on the surface looked pretty simple. All major banks offered the origination of ACH debits as a standard service. Major insurance companies had converted their large preauthorized bases, seemingly without too much trouble, to ACH transactions.

However, beneath the surface existed significant challenges for corporations. First, the actual capture of the banking data to route transactions wasn't as simple as it seemed. The data needed was on the bottom of the consumer's check in the MICR line. However, banks had implemented their account number systems inconsistently. It wasn't clear from bank to bank whether dashes or spaces were needed. Sometimes there were branch codes and transaction codes buried in the account line. In addition, there was an issue around credit unions and their use of "payable thru" drafts containing data that was not accurate for ACH transactions.

Second, it was not that easy for corporations to generate ACH files for consumer payments. Most corporations had developed their own internal consumer accounts receivable systems. If they wanted to use the ACH, they needed to add to the consumer database a bank routing transit number, a bank account number, and transaction codes, as well as create the process to generate a recurring ACH payment file and update the receivable file to show the consumer paid in full. When confronted with this project, the IT staffs often viewed this as a major rewrite of the receivables system that was going to be expensive.

There were also other issues negatively impacting corporations. It was unclear how many consumers would actually sign up if offered the service. Marketing of the service was virtually nonexistent. The only marketing to date in this area had been around signing up employees for direct deposit of paychecks. Additionally, the legal framework for consumers was just getting established. There were ongoing concerns around what protection companies were providing for consumers.

So CheckFree went to work at solving theses issues for corporate clients.

To capture bank and checking account data accurately, we built our own financial institution file (FIF). The file contained the basic bank routing information, but as we received returns, we'd build additional data edits around each financial institution. Our FIF over a relatively long timeframe became pretty sophisticated, allowing us to accurately know and manage the inconsistencies among banks. We also were able to successfully build edits that allowed us to manage the credit unions' "payable thru" issue accurately.

To overcome the issues that companies encountered in their own back offices, we developed the ability to cross-reference the companies' consumer receivable databases and a database we managed that stored their respective banking and payment information. This allowed a company to just send us a payment file that contained the consumer's name, internal account number, payment and payment date. The company didn't need to rewrite its entire system. We then were able to effectively manage the origination of the ACH file.

Additionally, we provided implementation services to help manage the implementation internally at the company. We also provided marketing services for the initial launch as well as ongoing support to aid the company in signing up consumers.

We added credit card as a payment option and pioneered batch authorizations. We also launched some value-added returns processing, through which we could re-clear NSF transactions and provide significantly more support back to the company around return item activity. All this was provided to the company on a per-item basis, allowing a company to utilize the ACH system without making a significant upfront investment or taking on undue risk.

Videotext, Online Service Providers

The next big industry that CheckFree impacted was the video-text industry. The videotext industry had started out as a way for companies to offload their excess computer capacity with text information services and sell it to other corporations. This process was known commonly in those days as "timesharing." Companies evolved the process further and started to provide these same services directly to consumers. They wanted to charge consumers on a per-usage basis, but they struggled with how to collect payments from them. The initial approach had been to use a simple, back-office billing system. But it soon became clear that sending a bill out each month and waiting for the payment would not work for a consumer market. A company would be waiting for its payment while at the same time the consumer was running up additional charges. The company wouldn't know for several weeks whether this was its best customer about to pay them or its worst customer with no intention to pay.

By chance, Pete was on a flight with Jeff Wilkens, then the CEO of CompuServe, the leading online provider. Pete was able to talk to Jeff about the CheckFree service, and, within a few months, CheckFree was pioneering a solution for CompuServe. In signing up for the service, a consumer would sign an authorization to agree to utilize their checking or saving account for payment of his or her online-services bill. Since the account each month was automatically charged, the online-service provider knew within a few days whether or not the consumer had the money to pay for the service. As the industry evolved, we worked with it, innovating the enrollment, authorization, and collection processes.

Ultimately, the approach used at CompuServe was so successful that CheckFree became the standard way for the early Internet service providers to collect their consumer bills. We worked with

Delphi, Genie, and Quantum Computing. Quantum, of course, became better known after they changed their name to America Online. We also worked with the industry to switch to a flat monthly fee model, which is still widely used today.

By 1986, CheckFree's corporate service, as we came to call it, was a success. We had signed nearly a thousand health and fitness facilities and were processing for every major online service provider. We thought we had made it through the really challenging period of building a business. We were making money and thought it would be downhill from here. Boy, were we wrong.

Consumer Bill Pay

Prior to 1987, a few select banks had offered a rudimentary bill payment service. This had been done either through a phone or through an online PC product. The early bill payment services had a very limited number of consumers and were plagued by inconsistent quality. They were also very expensive for the banks to provide.

As a consumer, you needed to have an account with a bank offering the service. The interfaces tended to be online and clunky. The payment first came out of your bank account, and after the bank knew there were good funds, they then sent the funds to the biller to post. To the consumer, this meant that you incurred negative float. In addition, the number of actual billers that would receive payments electronically was very small, which meant most payments were sent as paper checks, adding to the delay in the consumer's account getting posted. In other words, as a consumer you had to really want to pay bills from your computer to use one of the services.

Pete, in or around 1986, became interested in providing a service directly to consumers to pay all of their bills. There were a couple of things that pushed him. First, he had become frustrated by how long it took a corporation to sign up for CheckFree's service. It took considerable time and energy to sign and implement a large corporation. And once we signed the corporation, it would have a major impact on the actual number of consumers who would sign up. If it marketed poorly, the sign-up rates would be as low as 1 to 2 percent. We had done enough independent consumer research to know that somewhere between 5 and 10 percent of a company's consumers would sign up for a preauthorized service if presented properly. We also knew from the research that the same 5 percent, if offered the opportunity, would elect to pay all of their bills automatically.

We decided to take a fresh look at what kinds of consumer bill payment services could be offered. After some research and a lot of prototyping, we decided to introduce a service different from what the banks had been offering. We felt that consumers paid bills as part of managing household money. We decided to base our product on the personal financial management (PFM) software model. We knew that the two leading PFM products at the time (Managing Your Money® and Intuit Quicken®) were growing well and decided to target that marketplace with a simplified version that included bill payment. The product we started to develop would not only allow a consumer to pay any bill but also track expenses and maintain a register that could be reconciled against a consumer's bank account. Given that it was application software, it made sense for us to design a batch transmission interface to minimize the cost of communications.

But the major innovation was to allow consumers to bank anywhere in the U.S. The consumer would sign up with CheckFree, and we would manage the debit from the consumer's account and the payment to the biller's account. This presented us with significant challenges. In utilizing the ACH system for debiting a consumer's account, we wouldn't know for a few days whether or not there were sufficient funds in the consumer's account to cover the debit. To mitigate this risk, we devised an approach in which we would manage individual payment risk by converting higher risk transactions to paper drafts. By doing this, we weren't a party to that transaction. Instead, we were in essence writing a check for the consumer.

To accomplish this, we needed to be able to decide whether we were willing to take risk on any given transaction and then appropriately generate an ACH debit or a paper draft with the accurate bank information. The FIF, which we had built, for the corporate business had a lot of the routing and account number data needed for switching between paper and electronic. To effectively manage the risk, we needed to build a credit management system. After developing and continually enhancing the system, we were able to create an effective approach to managing the risk. The system was unique, and as such we received a patent on the system we had devised.

We also believed that the service for the consumer should be "floatless," meaning the debit to the consumer's account should post the same date as the credit at the biller's account. Since we had to manage the payment risk anyway, why not make the product as consumer friendly as possible? So we built a three-day window into paying a bill so we could send the payments to the merchant earlier than the date of the ACH debit. By allowing the three-day window, we were able to get a sufficient number of payments posted the same date as the consumer debit. Additionally, this was similar to the way consumers thought about paying bills by check. Consumers mailed their payments typically prior to the due date and were accustomed to posting a few days afterward.

The other process we invented was an automated approach for receiving new merchants from the consumer via the personal computer. We automatically cross-referenced them with a merchant table to allow us to consolidate as many payments to the billers as possible to reduce our costs. In developing a product that we could market and provide nationwide, we were able to be more aggressive with billers to move to electronic receipt of payments given the continued and strong growth we were experiencing.

We started work in 1987 on the product and didn't launch it publicly until 1989. Within a couple weeks of launching the service, we were contacted by Intuit and Managing Your Money and developed commercial relationships with both to build a CheckFree interface into their products, allowing MYM and Quicken users to pay bills.

The product quickly enjoyed market success; however, it would take us some time to have financial success. The size and complexity of providing bill payment on a national basis with early PC technology was beyond any cost we had imagined. For the next three years, we lost money, year after year, and struggled to solve a never-ending list of problems.

We were pleasantly surprised however when, despite all the challenges in providing the service, consumers by and large loved it.

In some ways, the ACH system actually worked well for our form of consumer bill payment. The ACH system worked effectively nationwide with relatively consistent delivery. The batch nature of the ACH was consistent with the bill payment world, and the cost to utilize it was in line with what we could afford. The descriptions on the bank statements provided the consumer with an informative record.

Yet in other ways, the ACH system didn't work in our favor. The FIF had to become much more sophisticated. Problems occurred around whether or not pre-notes were required. Savings accounts and CMA (cash management accounts) were inconsistently handled by banks and brokerage houses. Returns were handled inconsistently from institution to institution. The ACH as a corporate crediting system was awful. Dollars flowed OK, but the accompanying data was problematic. There was a lack of flexibility in the formats, and forcing the data to go through the bank without an actual oversight body caused undue delay in getting payments posted at the biller. There was enough of an issue in this area that MasterCard was able to launch its RPS service even though it was simply a form of ACH.

By 1994, we were able to work our way through all the various issues to create a bill payment service that was marketed directly to consumers and could make money, but it was not ultimately the best way to acquire consumers.

The Acquisition of SSI (Servantis)

Larry Dean had started Stockholders System Inc., or SSI, in 1971 in Atlanta, Georgia. SSI had partnered with Trust Company of Georgia (now SunTrust) on an automated shareholder accounting system. In late 1974, Trust Company invited two SSI executives, Larry Dean and John Stephens, to a presentation on the ACH at the bank's offices. Trust Company was a participant in the new Georgia Automated Clearing House and had written a couple of programs to automate processing. GACHA was the third ACH to go live, after California and Maryland. (ACHs were statewide organizations in the beginning).

As the story goes, Larry and John liked what they heard about the new, automated way of transferring money. They were inspired. But the concept was still very new. Even though they were still trying to understand the opportunity, they could envision how the concept could be revolutionary for the banks. Immediately, the wheels began to turn, and they drove back to their office—a three-bedroom house in College Park, Georgia—to share the news with the company's eight other employees.

Starting with rudimentary programs from Trust Company, SSI began to develop a software product the banks could use to interface between corporations and the ACH system at the Federal Reserve. They called the initial software system "the Paperless Entry Processing," or, as it became better known, PEP. This became the predecessor for today's current PEP+ system, which is now used to process about two-thirds of all ACH transactions.

The PEP software product's first installation came in June 1975. Larry predicted he would sell ten units of the newly developed PEP product. However, SSI sold ten times that many within a year, taking a critical step toward becoming the leader in providing the ACH software utilized by the banking industry.

It wasn't long before SSI's clients began to ask about the new, touch-tone banking service—telephone bill pay. Audio response systems had been around for a while, but the idea of customers initiating bill payment transactions was pretty revolutionary then. In 1978, SSI enlisted eight PEP client banks as development partners and proceeded to develop PEP Telephone Teller, which went on to become the most widely accepted telephone bill payment software in domestic use.

SSI had gone through a number of changes in the 1980s and early 1990s. It had gone public and then was bought out by NYNEX (now Verizon). Later, NYNEX sold it to a private equity company: Welsh, Carson, Anderson & Stowe. Welsh Carson renamed it "Servantis."

Meanwhile, after going public on the NASDAQ in 1995, CheckFree began to look for potential companies to acquire and came across Servantis. Both companies knew of each other but seldom had much interaction. Servantis had just purchased a bill payment organization out of Austin, Texas, and was about to enter the marketplace. CheckFree, meanwhile, had begun to get inquiries from banks to provide a "white labeled" service that the bank could brand. Over the years, CheckFree had done a substantial amount of research, which consistently indicated that consumers expected to receive a bill payment service from their bank. However, CheckFree had little experience in selling to banks.

As the CheckFree management team dug deeper into Servantis's business, it was impressed with the depth of Serventis's bank relationships. The cornerstone of those relationships resulted from the widespread success of PEP in the electronic-operations area of the banks. After weeks of negotiating, CheckFree reached an agreement to acquire Servantis. Overnight, CheckFree became the leading provider of ACH software to the banking industry, as well as one of the largest users of the ACH service.

The Future

In going to work at CheckFree, I never doubted that the world would convert to electronic payments and that there would be significant business opportunities in helping this become a reality. The question was always how long it would take and if CheckFree would be able to survive and be a meaningful part of it. Looking back, I realize a number of significant trends have occurred that have helped CheckFree become a leader. They impact us still today and have implications for CheckFree as we look to the future.

First is the continued movement of paper electronification and whether it's a transaction or a financial process that is being displaced with an electronic alternative. All business and consumer processes are moving in this direction. CheckFree is a company founded on this trend. Look at CheckFree and the products we provide today. We provide ACH software to enable businesses and banks to move transactions to electronic formats. We provide bill payment services to allow consumers to replace their check payments. We provide bill presentment software and services to billers to eliminate their need to print and mail bills. To billers, we also provide an accounts receivable conversion (ARC) service that converts their lockbox payments to ACH transactions. In addition, we provide operational risk management software to banks, securities firms, and businesses that includes reconciliation capabilities to automate and electronify their reconciling and workflow processes. We provide walk-in payment capabilities; a consumer pays a bill in cash at a convenience counter, and we convert this to an electronic payment that is sent to the biller. Everywhere you look, CheckFree is creating and providing products to displace paper processes.

Another significant trend is the increasing size of the marketplace in which companies compete. Fifty years ago, businesses were local, and then they became regional and then national. Small hardware stores have given way to Home Depots. Independently owned bookstores have become novelties, while Barnes & Noble and Borders abound. And of course, you see this with banks. Local and regional banks have become national, and they continue to merge with each other—strengthening this trend in the banking industry every year. Bank customers expect to interact with their bank in any city, regardless of where it is based.

Without question, the next wave is global. In many industries, we have already seen this happen. Starbucks, Pizza Hut, Subway, BMW, Motorola, and McDonald's are showing up in all corners of the world, including in India, which is on the precipice of an economic boom. Wal-Mart CEO John Menzer was just there last year lobbying for foreign direct investment. Likewise, Aishwarya Rai, a popular actress in Bombay, recently promoted L'Oreal, DeBeers Diamonds, and Coca-Cola. Now we are seeing financial institutions becoming global. In the not-too-distant future, it won't be surprising to see your bank's name as visible on the streets of Paris, Tokyo, Hamburg, Salzburg, or Hong Kong as in your own hometown.

In conjunction with this, the payment world will have the ability to process and clear transactions throughout the world. We'll develop greater multicurrency capability, which will make it easy to move money from one country to another. This has already happened with credit cards and debit cards, which can easily be used internationally. Buy a second home in Spain, and pay its utility bills from your den in the U.S.

The third major trend has been the technology empowerment from the corporate level down to consumers. First it was the movement of computers from expensive corporate assets to personal computers that are affordable for almost any household. Then it was the movement of an expensive telecommunication network system to a virtually free Internet network. And now the movement is on to portable devices that wirelessly connect people and the corporations that serve them.

College libraries are going digital, and Wi-Fi brings the tools of the library to students anywhere on campus. Off campus, parents are keeping an eye on their kids through geopositioning technology. Many students now carry cell phones to relay data or have small devices that sit on the dashboards of their cars. The devices notify parents of speeding and show the location of the cars, at any time, via personal computers and the Internet.

"Mobile computing" will become a household term. You will manage transactions and handle electronic funds transfers from portable, handheld devices that you will carry with you everywhere. You are going to see a huge impact in the payment world from mobile telecommunications and mobile computing. Your wireless device will become your wallet. But even better than your current wallet, it will be able to provide you with your various, current credit card and checking account balances with a touch of the keypad.

I feel fortunate to have participated over the last thirty years in the dramatic changes that have occurred in the U.S. payment system. Without question, the trends I've outlined and others I've not even contemplated will continue to impact our payment systems dramatically over the next few decades. I also have confidence that CheckFree is well positioned to continue to innovate and define leading payment solutions to serve banks, billers, and consumers. And we thought the last thirty years were interesting.

(Note: Managing Your Money® is a registered trademark of MECA Software LLC. Quicken® is a registered trademark of Intuit Inc. Other parties' trademarks or service marks are the property of their respective owners and should be treated as such.)

Chapter 10

Contactless Payments and the Credit Card (R)evolution

Mohammad Khan, ViVOtech

You are speeding down the highway and hit a toll plaza. Do you stop the car, wait in line, and then exchange money with a live attendant? Not anymore. People in the know are finding that they can slow down and get a full accounting of their toll activity in one bill that has already been processed through their credit card company. And now you can do this with your morning coffee each morning and at the gas pump.

"Contactless" payments are a reality and already in the hands of millions of consumers, in the checkout lanes of thousands of merchants, and in numerous prime time advertising spots paid for by leading financial institutions. Backed by some of the most important players in the banking, payments, and retail sectors, contactless transactions are growing at an astounding pace, replacing cash as the most convenient method of payment available today. These cards, key fobs, and mobile phones allow consumers to quickly and easily pay for transactions with a tap or a wave. RF-based contactless payment devices are easy to use; consumers like the increased speed, control and security of transactions and are increasingly using the devices instead of cash. Retailers, too, are seeing better revenues as consumers spend more per transaction and purchase goods more frequently.

RF-based contactless payments are straightforward for both consumers and retailers. Consumers use a payment card or a key fob that is equipped with a chip and antenna that securely communicate consumer account information via radio frequency to the retailer's payment terminal. The payment terminal then connects to the appropriate financial networks or other back-end processing systems to authorize the transaction. Once authorized, the consumer completes the transaction in a fraction of the time required by cash or by traditional credit or debit transactions, which typically require a card to be swiped through a reader.

To date, all major card companies and Networks have started their own contactless payment programs. In 2002, MasterCard announced its contactless payments pilot of MasterCard PayPass™ in Orlando, Florida, with sixteen thousand cards issued by Chase,

Citibank, and MBNA. Over three hundred merchant locations were enabled in Orlando to accept PayPass-enabled contactless payments. Visa first tested contactless payments in 2002, working with Finland's Nordea Bank and Nokia on a mobile pilot. Also in 2002, American Express began a pilot for ExpressPay in Arizona and, New York. The success of these pilots led to the national launch of Blue from American Express® with the ExpressPay feature in June 2005.

In 2003, MasterCard and Nokia unveiled a PayPass-enabled mobile-phone trial in Dallas, Texas. Nokia mobile phones were enabled with Chase payment information stored on a PayPass-enabled RF chip embedded into the back cover of the phone. This trial was positively received by both consumers and merchants.

As momentum built for contactless technologies, the industry saw large scale commercial rollouts of Visa contactless programs in Malaysia in 2004 and in the US in 2005. Since mid-2005, both American Express and MasterCard have been driving the commercial rollout of their contactless programs. And Discover Network, a business unit of Discover Financial Services LLC, too, has now entered into contactless payments starting mid-2006. In just four short years, all of the major bankcard companies have moved to contactless payments as the result of customer demand.

Current moves in contactless payment include JPMorgan Chase's issue of approximately one million contactless credit cards per market in Atlanta, Denver, Orlando, Boston, Philadelphia, and New York in 2005 and in the first quarter of 2006. The bank expects to continue issuing contactless cards throughout 2006 in key demographic areas. Other issuers adopting contactless strategies include MBNA, Citibank, HSBC, KeyBank, Peoples Bank, and Citizens Bank – all issuing contactless credit, debit, and prepaid cards to their cardholders in 2006. More financial institutions are expected to follow suit with Wells Fargo's announcement that it will start issuing its credit cards with contactless technology.

As of June 2006, over fourteen million contactless credit, debit, and prepaid cards have been issued in the United States. ABI Research, a global research organization based in New York and founded in 1990 to assist manufacturers of wireless semiconductor components in understanding and entering new markets, expects that "forty million contactless cards, mini-cards, and fobs will ship globally in 2006."

As contactless payments are relatively new in the marketplace, American Express, MasterCard, and Visa worked together to create a universal Contactless Symbol for use on contactless payment readers and terminals. Its purpose is to help consumers understand how and where to tap their contactless card of device when it is time to pay. The Contactless Symbol is used in addition to the contactless payment brands accepted at the terminal.

Helping speed deployment at the consumer level, all of the associations are using the same technology standards for contactless payments to guarantee future interoperability. And usage of the cards or devices is similar between the different programs:

- A consumer is issued a contactless credit card that includes a contactless interface to an on-card chip and a magnetic stripe. Track 1 (T1) and/or Track 2 (T2) magnetic stripe data (cardholder name, card number, and expiration date) and other security information is stored in the chip.

- Retailers connect the radio frequency-based reader devices to existing POS terminals, ECRs, and PC-based systems.

- The consumer holds the contactless card or device in close proximity to a specially equipped terminal. The card communicates unique payment account information wirelessly to the terminal via radio frequency, providing the information needed to complete the transaction and eliminating the need for the cardholder to hand a card to the merchant to swipe.

- The terminal processes the payment as it would a traditional magnetic-stripe credit card transaction, sending the account information and transaction amount to the appropriate acquiring processor for authorization. No changes are required of the retailer or acquirer systems for authorization and settlement.

- Upon transaction authorization, the consumer receives payment confirmation and completes the transaction. For many low-cost retail purchases (e.g., fast food, theater tickets, or parking), a signature may not be required, making the checkout process even faster.

- Considering unique payment account information is produced by the contactless card every time, it can not be replayed for fraudulent use.

As of June 2006, there are over 30,000 merchant locations representing over 180,000 POS locations that accept contactless credit, debit, and prepaid cards in the United States. Brand-name retailers such as McDonalds, 7-Eleven, KFC, Regal Theaters, United Artist Theaters, CVS Pharmacy, Meijer, Sheetz Petroleum, Ritz Camera, and Arby's have enabled their store locations nationwide to start accepting contactless payments.

The launch of RF-enabled credit cards has seen unprecedented support from card associations and issuers. MasterCard started running national television advertising in late 2005, leveraging their renowned "Priceless" format to introduce MasterCard PayPass to US consumers, and continues to actively support it using a variety of regional and national media including billboards, transit boards, and bus shelter and newspaper advertising. JPMorgan Chase is supporting its contactless efforts by running multimedia advertising in a market-by-market strategy. In addition to television commercials for their "Blink" contactless card product. Visa, American Express, and MasterCard all feature contactless technology benefits prominently on their respective Web sites.

Contactless Goes Global

Contactless technology is growing worldwide as an added feature of the EMV smart card outside of United States. Several countries in Asia and the Pacific including Australia, India, Japan, Korea, Malaysia, the Philippines, Taiwan, and Thailand now have deployments of contactless payment technology. In fact, tens of thousands of merchants are already enabled with contactless technology in Asia. MasterCard is deploying its contactless EMV program under the name of OneSmart® MasterCard PayPass™ in all of these countries, whereas Visa is rolling out its contactless EMV-based solution in some of these countries under the brand name Visa Wave™.

Europe, the Middle East, and Africa have been catching up too, with a number of early deployments of contactless EMV systems underway. In early 2006, MasterCard International announced deployment of its OneSmart MasterCard PayPass program with Royal Bank of Scotland. A dual-interface card, typically referred to as a "combi card," that supports both contact and contactless EMV applications on the same card will be issued by Royal Bank of Scotland in the United Kingdom. As a low-cost and attractive alternative to cash, a cardholder will be able to just tap his or her "combi card" on a contactless reader for a transaction below fifteen pounds; for a purchase with a higher amount, a consumer will insert the card into a smart-card reader, as is typically done in the UK. Further deployments in larger quantities are expected during second half of 2006. Additional rollouts of contactless EMV solutions are also expected in Latin America by the end of the year.

Retailers Going with Contactless Prepaid, Gift Card, and Loyalty

Interest in contactless technology is also coming from retailers who want to have their own prepaid or loyalty program. In March of 2006, the Smoothie King franchise chain was the first to announce such a program in the U.S. Smoothie King's Denver-area stores implemented a MiFare-based, contactless, prepaid card program with contactless key fobs and readers provided by Silicon Valley-based ViVOtech. In a survey of the initial program, 94 percent of participants who responded reported favoring the convenience of the fob form factor, and nearly 60 percent stated that they would be "very likely" to load their prepaid-enabled key fobs again.

ViVOtech has also developed the ViVOplatform processing software application for retailers to manage contactless prepaid, gift, and loyalty card programs, offering retailers an end-to-end solution. These developments are only leading to more deployments of contactless loyalty and prepaid programs launching this year in the U.S. and abroad.

A Common Symbol for All Contactless Readers

A universal contactless acceptance symbol has been agreed to by all major card associations for use on a contactless reader:

This symbol is placed in the middle of a contactless reader's antenna, indicating the spot to tap or wave a contactless device to make a payment.

Contactless – Can Mean Cardless

Key Fob Payments

Once consumers have a contactless fob placed on their key chains, they may have a higher tendency to use contactless payments for purchases every time instead of reaching into their wallets or purses to get their payment cards. This convenience ensures a "top-of-the-wallet" effect for a card issuer. This is what one major card issuer, Citibank, has decided to do. Citibank is currently issuing contactless key fobs to its credit and debit account holders in the New York area, expecting to enjoy higher usage of its payment contactless device than other cards its cardholders might be carrying at the time of purchase.

NFC Mobile-Phone Payments

Further fueling the adoption of contactless technology is Near Field Communication (NFC) mobile-phone payments. NFC is the name of contactless technology adapted by the mobile-phone industry, and it is backward compatible to contactless radio frequency technology standards adopted by the payment industry. Erik Michielsen, director of ABI Research's RFID and M2M practices forecasts that, "By 2010, more than 50 percent of cellular handsets—some five hundred million units—will incorporate NFC capabilities1." Over five hundred million people will be able to access contactless payments via their cell phones.

ViVOtech has tapped into this market with the development of payment software for NFC mobile phones to allow consumers to make payments at the same contactless readers being deployed by the payment industry. Since ViVOtech's first pilot rollout last December in Atlanta with industry leaders Visa USA, Cingular, Chase, Nokia, Philips, and Atlanta Spirit interest in NFC payments has been growing exponentially. In April 2006 in Malaysia, Visa, May Bank, Maxis, and Nokia announced the first NFC pilot with Mobile Visa Wave payment. Both of the highly visible NFC pilots are attracting the attention of several organizations that have been slower to adapt contactless technology.

[1.]   ABI Research Press Release: Oyster Bay, NY. May 23, 2006.

With the deep penetration of mobile phones in Asia and other regions, the availability of contactless payments may portend a huge shift in the way consumers pay for goods and services in those cultures. While these initiatives represent real and present revenue opportunity for all players involved, they are currently segregated by region or functionally from one another. New global products need to be developed today with an eye to interoperability so that mobile-phone payments can be a success tomorrow.

NFC mobile-phone payment will also affect the activation of an "unbanked" consumer base worldwide to start using electronic payments for purchases at physical as well as online stores. Over the last few years, hundreds of millions of people without relationships with banks have started using prepaid mobile phones around the world. It should be no surprise when these customers also start paying with prepaid mobile phones, especially when such phones start becoming available with NFC technology.

Traditional Credit and Debit Card Payment

Most of the focus in initial contactless payment pilots has been on using RF-based payment cards or key fobs to enhance value to existing credit and debit cards. This application has tremendous potential for high-traffic and cash-dominant retail segments where transaction speed is essential and cash replacement is desirable. Quick-service restaurants (QSR), convenience stores, gas stations, theaters, grocery stores, and parking facilities are typical retailers who are benefiting from the technology.

Contactless payments are proven to provide faster transactions times, increased ticket size, and greater customer loyalty. Nothing trades hand and consumers merely tap their contactless payment devices, like cards, key fobs, or mobile phones, on a contactless reader to complete a payment. This feeling of control provides consumers with a sense of of security while also paying faster and with greater convenience. The simplicity of making a purchase under twenty-five dollars has improved dramatically as a consumer does not even need sign or enter a PIN number for most transactions.

In worldwide contactless payment trials, consumers have responded favorably to the new payment cards and processes. Consumers report that they enjoy using their contactless cards. In fact, MasterCard's consumer feedback indicated that PayPass was perceived to be "fun to use" and made shopping "less of a hassle." American Express, too, reports that focus group research shows that consumers like the new payment device and are excited about its ease of use.

Contactless payment provides the following tangible retailer benefits:

- Replacement of cash
- Faster transaction processing
- Increased size and frequency of transactions
- Improved access to customer data
- Improved transaction security

Replacement of cash. Cash and checks make up 58 percent of the six trillion dollars worth of consumer payments in the U.S. The Nilson Report estimates that within five years cash and checks will represent less than 37 percent of all transactions, with cards representing over 49 percent. Contactless payment implementations are becoming one of the main drivers of this trend, enabling consumers to pay with RF-based credit cards more easily than with cash.

The top fifty QSR chains in the U.S. are expected to generate more than eighty-seven billion dollars in sales throughout 100,000 locations. However, though many U.S. fast-food restaurants accept credit cards, they have been mostly corporate-owned stores, and many franchisees are just now embracing credit. McDonald's has taken the lead in accepting credit and debit cards and has rolled out contactless payment systems at all US locations. Conversion of fast-food customers to RF-based contactless payment offers tremendous value to the retailer by eliminating cash handling, saving time and improving convenience..

Faster transaction processing. RF-based contactless payments speed transaction times at checkout. Consumers are not required to extract cash or cards for purchases, and retailers are not required to give change or swipe a card. Transaction time is even further reduced in certain retail segments (such as QSRs, movie theaters, and parking lots) where card associations no longer require signatures if transactions are below certain dollar limits. This results in increased profits as retailers can more efficiently handle a larger number of customers, vital during peak periods. Multiple studies done by card associations have shown that contactless payment is more than 50 percent faster than both cash and cards.

Increased size and frequency of transactions. Studies and early implementations of contactless payment have shown that consumers spend more if they are not required to use cash and that they frequent retailers who offer convenience and quick checkout with less hassle. Numerous implementations have resulted in increases of up to 30 percent in sales for retailers accepting RF-based contactless payment.

Improved access to customer data. Cash sales are anonymous, providing retailers with no information about their customers. Using RF-based contactless payment, retailers can collect data about customer buying habits and preferences. By making the cash customer purchases visible, retailers can better understand customer behavior and implement targeted promotions to further increase sales and extend customer loyalty.

Improved transaction security. Contactless smart cards provide a highly secure payment solution. Consumer account information is stored securely on the chip, and the cards themselves are tamper-resistant and extremely difficult to duplicate. A payment transaction initiated by the contactless smart card's built-in chip is considered much more secure than one initiated with a magnetic stripe card.

The major international card companies—MasterCard, Visa, and American Express—have launched rollouts offering RF-based contactless payment devices. All of the implementations have been based on technology complying with the ISO 14443 standard. This strong financial industry support, coupled with the favorable consumer reaction and strong retailer benefits demonstrated in early implementations, is expected to motivate issuers to offer new RF-based payment cards.

Retailer Implementation and Benefits of Contactless Payment

For a new payment technology to be successful in the market, retailers must implement the infrastructure required to accept and process payments. Payment technologies such as EMV contact smart cards require significant investment by retailers and payment processors, and market deployment is slow while the infrastructure is upgraded over time.

Retailers can quickly and easily implement contactless payment and start accepting contactless payment cards and key fobs being issued by card associations. This is facilitated by the payment approach being implemented and by the products being offered, which allow retailers to adapt existing POS systems to accept contactless payment cards.

- In U.S. pilot implementations of contactless payment, elements of T1 and T2 magnetic stripe data and other data is stored in the contactless card. The card then communicates T1 and T2 payment account information and sometimes other data to the terminal via radio frequency. In order to accept contactless payment, the POS must be able to "read" specific security information inherent to contactless credit cards and pass the information to the payment processing network. All of the major acquirers and processors have completed all software changes in their "back end" to process contactless transactions. Many POS hardware and software vendors have also completed the data element changes required by Visa and MasterCard, resulting in over thirty thousand merchant locations now accepting contactless credit cards. Category leaders such as McDonald's, 7-Eleven, CVS Pharmacy, and

Regal Cinemas are examples. American Express doesn't require any additional data elements to be passed.

- Vendors are offering RF-based terminals that can be installed quickly and easily with existing POS systems. With solutions available that permit retailers to upgrade POS systems while also retaining existing functionality, contactless payment acceptance is straightforward and inexpensive for retailers to implement. By basing contactless payments on the existing magnetic stripe payment infrastructure, major card associations have launched programs that are driving more rapid acceptance of contactless payment cards by retailers—similar to the growth seen by gift-card programs that used existing infrastructure. This approach and the innovative products being offered by terminal vendors allow retailers to realize the significant benefits of accepting contactless payment cards with minimal investment.

Opportunities for Acquirers and ISOs

The emergence of RF-based contactless payment technology provides acquirers and independent sales organizations (ISOs) with the opportunity to differentiate product and service offerings, gain additional revenue, and help their retail customers take advantage of the benefits of RF-based contactless payment.

- **Increased revenue**. Early market results show that retailers can easily start accepting Visa Contactless, MasterCard PayPass, and ExpressPay from American Express[SM] contactless payment cards. By offering low-cost terminal solutions and helping retailers with the straightforward POS installation, acquirers and ISOs can quickly increase revenue from equipment sales and monthly leases or rentals and gain share in this emerging market.

- **Higher transaction fees through more and bigger transactions**. Through early rollouts, it has been established that consumers tend to pay at least 20 percent more often with contactless than with cash, driving more transactions; equally, consumers tend to spend at least 20 percent more when using contactless rather than cash, driving bigger transactions Acquirers and ISOs will see an increase in card usage by consumers with contactless payment cards. This means higher transaction fee revenue for ISOs and acquirers.

- **Increased penetration of traditional cash-only retail segments**. By offering RF-based contactless payment solutions, acquirers and ISOs can better serve traditional cash-only retail segments that need fast transaction processing. By upgrading payment systems at QSRs, parking facilities, movie theaters, and other retailers to accept RF-based contactless payment, acquirers and ISOs can increase transaction volume (converting cash to credit transactions) and gain additional revenue from equipment purchases.

- **New value-added service portfolio**. RF-based contactless transactions are not limited to payments. The emergence of this new technology provides opportunities for acquirers and ISOs to add to their portfolios new services that can differentiate their offerings from retailers. Offering outsourced loyalty, prepaid-card, or electronic-coupon services can help acquirers and ISOs develop new sources of revenues.

- **Better return on existing POS investment**. Acquirers and ISOs will be able to enjoy an extension in the lifetime of their existing POS terminal installed base, providing revenue over a longer period of time.

Acquirers and ISOs can quickly and easily capitalize on this new market opportunity by offering retailers a straightforward upgrade to their POS equipment to accept RF-based contactless payment devices.

RF-Based Payment Technologies

A number of technologies can be used to implement contactless payment systems. Key RF-based technologies include:

1. ISO 14443-compliant RF contactless smart-card technology

2. RFID token-based solutions

3. Sony FeliCa smart-card technology

4. Near field communications (NFC)

ISO 14443-Compliant RF Contactless Smart-Card Technology

Standards are important for the adoption of technology, as they provide the ability to base multiple sources of products on the same standard. The ISO has standardized the technologies used in contactless smart cards. Contactless smart cards compliant with the ISO 14443 international standard for contactless cards are used in numerous payment applications, with over 200 million cards in use worldwide. Contactless payment cards based on ISO 14443 communicate with readers at 13.56 MHz and have an operational range of up to ten centimeters (approximately four inches). Operational range is the maximum distance between the proximity card and reader for reading and writing data to and from the card. The ISO 14443 standard provides an option for two different types of signaling schemes.

Both signaling schemes offer half-duplex communication with a data rate of 106 kilobits per second in each direction and use a sub-carrier modulation frequency of 847.5 KHz to transmit data. An ISO 14443 card is powered by the RF field and does not require its own battery.

Applications based on ISO 14443 A/B are highly secure when compared to those using magnetic stripe cards and other RF-based technologies. Counterfeit cards are extremely difficult to manufacture, and the cards themselves are tamper resistant. Built-in security features on the contactless card allow the encryption of data on the card during communication with the POS terminal and prevent the "replay" of transactions. Contactless smart cards now achieve the same degree of security as contact smart cards.

All major card associations are endorsing the ISO 14443 standard, with RF-based contactless payment initiatives using the technology. ViVOtech readers have firmware that accepts MasterCard, Visa, and American Express contactless cards at the same reader.

ExpressPay from American Express, Discover Network Contactless, MasterCard PayPass, and Visa Contactless use ISO 14443 types A/B to communicate T1 and T2 magnetic stripe credit card data from the contactless card to the retailer's POS terminal. This critical decision assured a worldwide, interoperable payment system based on RF contactless technology. Retailers can easily add a compatible RF reader to existing certified POS systems.

RFID Token-Based Solutions

RFID token-based solutions are typically used in closed payment systems. Applications in North America include automated toll collection and payment services for gas stations and convenience stores (e.g., Exxon Mobil Speedpass). In an RFID token-based system, a unique ID is stored on the RF-based consumer key fob. This ID is transmitted via RF (either low or high frequency) to the receiver where it is sent to a central processing system. The central processing system then links the consumer ID to a payment account, and payment is completed (either through a pre-funded account or through standard credit card processing).

RFID token-based systems can operate at longer ranges—0.2 to 10 meters (approximately 0.75 to 33 feet) depending on the frequency—increasing their attractiveness for certain contactless payment applications (e.g., toll collection). To date, they have not received any support from the financial industry since they are perceived to have security risks and are based on proprietary technology with no global standard. Systems that use RFID tokens may require a separate processing infrastructure, and retailers may incur additional costs for processing transactions.

Sony FeliCa

Over thirty-five million Sony FeliCa contactless smart cards have been issued worldwide, including large-scale implementations in Hong Kong, Singapore, and Japan. Sony FeliCa technology is used throughout Asia Pacific for transit, electronic purse, and loyalty applications. The proprietary Sony FeliCa cards use 13.56 MHz to communicate with readers. Sony FeliCa technology has similar technical specifications to ISO 14443 A/B but is not compliant with the standard.

JCB has also announced a contactless smart card that incorporates both Sony FeliCa contactless and EMV contact technology and will be used for JCB employees as both an ID and a payment card. Sony is also working with Visa and Infineon to develop a common chip supporting ISO 14443 A/B and FeliCa technology.

NFC

Near field communication (NFC) is a very short-range frequency identification (RFID) protocol that provides easy and secure communications among various devices without user configuration. NFC range is measured in centimeters, which provides just enough range for end users to leverage the technology's intuitive, easy-to-use nature to transfer content among devices, make payment transactions, and access content from smart objects.

NFC devices recognize each other in short-range scenarios and, regardless of manufacturer, transmit data to enhance user functionality. Some proponents see NFC as transforming consumer lifestyle and building the bridge across the consumer electronics, communications, and computing islands that exist today.

NFC technology is compatible with ISO 14443 Type A, Type B, and Felica RF-enabled devices. This means NFC devices can work with contactless readers being deployed as part of contactless programs initiated by American Express, MasterCard, and Visa, as well as NTT Docomo and Sony.

To date, NFC-driven demonstrations have included digital music transfers, smart-poster interaction, boarding-ticket transfers, electronic key access, mobile-phone payment at physical stores, and interactive-service electronic payments. NFC technology is bolstered by strong ISO and ECMA standards, and the technology is generating interest and action across multiple industry leaders. Nokia, Motorola, Samsung, and LG have shown early models of their mobile phones with NFC technology. In late 2005, Nokia released a production-quality NFC option for its Nokia 3220 mobile phones. This model with ViVOtech wallet payment software is being used in multiple field pilots in the United States and Asia for mobile-phone payment and reading smart-poster applications.

POS Solution

Vendors are offering contactless RF readers that can quickly and easily be installed as part of existing POS systems. In the future, POS terminal vendors are also expected to release new POS terminals with physically integrated contactless readers—especially for the consumer-operated payment terminal market.

An RF contactless reader can be easily interfaced to existing POS systems using serial cable interfaces. A small software modification is made on the POS system to talk to the contactless reader and to provide a flag in transaction data so that a bank authorization system can establish that it is a contactless transaction and process it accordingly.

ViVOtech has developed a suite of contactless readers that fit merchants' varying POS environments (e.g., in-store registers, drive-thru windows, vending machines, table-service restaurants, and kiosks). ViVOtech also developed customer brackets that "visually integrate" its ViVOpay 4000 to a POS device. As counter space in most retailers is limited, the ability to add a contactless reader without increasing the terminal footprint is important.

NFC Infrastructure Solution

In 2005, ViVOtech announced the industry's first end-to-end near field communication (NFC) payment solution. The ViVOnfc solution provides a secure infrastructure to accelerate the adoption and usage of NFC-enabled mobile phones.

With ViVOnfc, users with NFC phones will be able to carry their credit and debit cards virtually and make contactless payments at merchant locations. NFC technology provides short-range wireless connectivity over a typical distance of just two to four inches. Since NFC devices do not operate over a carrier's radio spectrum, they can be used anywhere.

Designed specifically to meet the stringent security and encryption requirements of the payments industry, ViVOtech's end-to-end NFC Contactless solution package includes:

- **ViVOprovisioning** Server is an over-the-air (OTA) provisioning infrastructure, which allows issuers to securely download a variety of "soft cards" over the carrier's radio spectrum into NFC phones. These include credit, debit, prepaid, loyalty, and gift cards. This server-based software was developed for both card issuers and cell-phone operators, i.e., VpIS and VpCS.

- **ViVOwallet software** turns mobile devices into secure consumer payment and promotion devices. ViVOwallet gives customers secure access to their credit, debit, promotions, and gift/stored-value cards in real time for purchase at retailers. A customer simply waves his or her mobile phone at a cash register enabled with the ViVOpay reader, and the preselected card is transferred via NFC or other contactless technology to the merchant for a contactless payment transaction. Contactless payments allow the ViVOwallet to operate everywhere, even in locations without mobile-phone coverage, such as inside shopping malls and in rural areas. ViVOwallet enables customers to carry multiple cards effortlessly and gives them more savings opportunities by allowing them to participate in as many merchant loyalty programs as they want. This software also provides transaction reporting functions to transmit balances, history, service discovery, and electronic coupons.

- **ViVOpaylet software package** provides secure communications between the NFC phone and the growing number of merchant locations that are being equipped to accept contactless payments. More than a hundred thousand ViVOtech contactless payment readers have been installed in fast-food restaurants, convenience stores, drug stores, drive-thru retailers, and gas stations.

The Future of Consumer Spending

Market momentum is building for RF-based contactless payments. With the contactless payment initiatives launching from all major card associations and networks, along with the positive results achieved in early implementations, RF-based contactless payment solutions are starting to deploy quickly both nationally and in specific geographic markets across the globe where contactless cards are being issued and embraced by consumers.

The value proposition for all participants in a contactless payment transaction is clear. Consumers enjoy increased convenience and faster checkout times. Retailers can quickly and easily take advantage of this emerging new payment technology to speed transaction processing, increase revenue, and better understand customer buying behavior. With RF-based contactless smart cards, transactions are more secure and the technology's multi-application capability allows retailers, acquirers, and issuers to implement creative new programs (e.g., RF-based contactless implementations of loyalty programs, prepaid/gift cards, and other single- or multiple-retailer promotion programs). The replacement of cash with RF-based contactless credit card payment also allows acquirers and issuers to increase transaction volume and revenue. The case for contactless payment is clear—in the present and the future.

Chapter 11

Additional Views on Emerging Changes

11.1 The Electronic Check Sorting Diet
Clint Shank, SortLogic Systems

Bankers will gain a lot of efficiencies from Check 21.
Now every paper pass beyond prime capture, including fine
sorts **and statement sorts, can be done electronically. Here's
how to** eliminate those paper passes today and achieve a
leaner, more profitable operation.

How much does it cost your operation every time someone
handles a paper check? Do you know? Do you care? You should.
While your check-processing operations may appear to be more
efficient than ever, that doesn't mean you shouldn't be concerned
about how much paper check handling, especially secondary
sort passes, is costing you. Almost invisibly, those costs may be
bleeding you.

In the early days of check automation, prime pass capture was the focus. The goal was to capture as many checks as quickly as possible, perform one or more secondary passes to break down the items to their final endpoints, and worry later about how to make the process more efficient.

Now it is later.

For certain, remote deposit capture is cutting a lot of fat from the cost of check processing. Check image exchange promises additional savings and efficiencies. But most banks still haven't extracted some of the easiest dollar savings of all. The bottom-line battlefield is beginning to move to all of the paper handling that occurs after prime pass capture whether it's a check or a new-fangled image replacement document (IRD).

And tools enabled by Check 21 are the weapons of choice.

Spurred by the desire to find any and every way possible to reduce operations costs, many banks have begun to do the math and are ready to make changes to decrease costs—and risk for error—that they incur every time they handle checks and IRDs. From moving work between stations, manually loading transport feeders, and performing fine sorts and statement sorts to dropping check trays, pulling the wrong trays, and misplacing batches, check handling drives up operations costs. IRDs are carrying these costs into the emerging Check 21 environment.

The savings are out there.

The solution is to use new virtual capture technology enabled by Check 21.

These software components provide any capture application with the ability to import prime pass images in one of the major check formats (x9.37, COFF, SWIFT). What's more, since they can also accept data from a capture system's archive or repository, they can also eliminate secondary paper passes. The software requires no changes to the bank's existing infrastructure and can be implemented in parallel with existing paper flows.

The software operates exactly like one of the bank's existing check sorters and appears to legacy capture applications as the same type of sorters running in the operation; the check-processing control system can't tell the difference. Virtual capture software feeds code-line data and images into the existing capture application and even supplies virtual control documents. Items can be rejected if their image quality falls short of predefined thresholds.

Checks are sorted electronically. The result is an end to secondary paper passes, providing more efficient day-one processing, lower operations costs, and an easier migration path to check image exchange.

And don't think such changes are just for big banks. Any bank could benefit by reducing paper handling and eliminating secondary passes. High volumes make the payoff bigger. But the move to virtual capture technology will provide benefits across all banks and get the industry one step closer to electronic check clearing.

11.2 Remote Deposit: Don't Do It Half-baked
Wally Vogel, Creditron Corporation

Remote deposit is garnering much attention and rightly so. The ability to electronically deposit checks rather than physically transporting them to the bank is a major step forward in banking. The deposit is only half of the work in processing incoming payments, though. The other half is applying the payment to accounts receivable. The ideal solution is to implement an integrated system for both remote deposit and cash application.

As a solution provider driven by innovation, Creditron has done considerable research into automated cash application. We have investigated the areas for opportunity in labor savings and worked with customers in various industries to develop and deliver image and recognition technology, as well as intuitive business rules software. In the process, we have learned much about the potential benefits.

In surveying payment processors, we have found that the cash application process is the more difficult process to automate, but it is the most rewarding. By utilizing check scanners together with recognition technology, historical databases, customer and invoice matching algorithms, and distributed data entry from image, the amount of time spent posting invoices can be significantly reduced. We have found that typically 60 percent of payments can be applied fully automatically—even taking into account factors such as discounts, credits, and returns. The balance can be applied with less effort using the image and assisted balancing with the posted amount, the payment amount, and difference shown. Other convenient posting features include the ability to create credits online and a feature that merges invoices from various sub-accounts when a head office payment is received and needs to be applied across multiple branches.

The net effect of the automated cash application has proven to be an incremental labor saving of 76 percent over and above the benefits of remote deposit alone. This savings ratio has been proven in a wide range of sites, from those processing only a few dozen checks per day to sites processing thousands of checks per day. The industries served have also varied greatly—from a shoe distributor to a major international courier company. We have learned that each business has slightly differing requirements, but once the business rules have been sufficiently evolved through multiple implementations, they are applicable universally.

When considering the move to remote deposit, look at the potential savings from automated cash application as well. Then you will be able to realize the full benefit of image based payment processing.

11.3 Have It Your Way
Gary Provo, eGistics

**On-demand technology lets you get
at the payments-related images and data you need—
when and how you want it.**

Nine years ago, Check 21 was still a pipedream, electronic payments were in their infancy, and eGistics Inc. was working on a new blend of technology and process. The Dallas-based company hatched a concept to let financial services organizations archive, manage, and deliver images and data over the Internet or dedicated communications lines. As images and data were captured, they were loaded into eGistics' digital infrastructure, where customized business rules and workflow processes were applied, and the information was made available to users when and how they wanted it. With this innovation, eGistics was among the first to hit on a concept that is now known as on-demand image and data archival, management, and delivery.

Fast-forward to today. Check 21 and electronic payments have become the next big things. End users and vendors alike are trying to develop and implement the type of distributed image and data functionality that eGistics pioneered and still uses. While imaging and ACH check conversion have recently become hot market categories, some of the companies that have successfully implemented electronic-payments frameworks have done so by looking beyond their back-office operations to on-demand applications. Market demands will keep this trend going.

The point of Check 21 and electronic payments is to automate and ultimately improve a company's financial supply chain. On-demand technology is a critical component of this process. If a company needs distributed image and data capture, it tends to need distributed archival, management, and delivery. If a company must support multiple payment channels—whether paper based or electronic—it should create a consolidated platform for managing the related images and data. If companies want to automate the processing of supplemental remittance documents—invoices, loan documents, explanation of benefits (EOBs), and such—they probably want to integrate these images and data with those from their payments.

The good news is that sophisticated on-demand services can help automate and streamline Check 21 and electronic-payments initiatives—as well as provide a flexible framework to support a larger menu of financial services applications. Even better, unlike the glut of packaged, stand-alone archival solutions, on-demand services are integrated so that companies can respond to the convergence of check and document processing, as to paper and electronic-payment channels. And innovation continues to push development of the market.

Companies are starting to realize that image and data archival, management, and delivery isn't a stand-alone element of individual Check 21 and electronic-payment initiatives, and it's not something to leave as an afterthought. It can lead companies to new levels of business automation; several on-demand projects have already produced notably successful results.

And time is of the essence because companies that establish on-demand infrastructures are getting a jump on developing a framework that supports Check 21 and electronic payments.

Gary Provo is executive vice president at Dallas-based eGistics Inc., which pioneered the use of on-demand image and data archival, management, and delivery for financial services applications. He can be reached at 214-256-4613 or via e-mail at gprovo@egisticsinc.com.

11.4 Check Recognition–Not a Commodity
Joe Gregory, Orbograph

Check recognition is not a commodity because few providers focus on check recognition as toolkit instead of as a line of business. Multiple POD variables including document mix, sorter image quality, teller validations, definitions, and confidence settings cause recognition rates to lag for many end users. We believe this is a clear illustration that the market has evolved into two distinct segments regarding price and performance.

Product offerings are distinguished based on read rate, accuracy, functionality, scalability, and price. Several major financial institutions have purchased commodity toolkit solutions for distributed systems and received a 70 percent read rate. Meanwhile, higher performing products attain 80 to 90 percent recognition when variables are optimized, resulting in savings of \$250,000 to \$500,000 per year per million items processed per day. The table below compares the two recognition segments:

Value-Based Solution Attributes	Commodity Driven "Toolkit"
• Robust application features	• Recognition engine, developer approach
• Scalable architecture supporting multiple applications	• Check-processing application handles load leveling
• Enterprise-oriented solution	• Reco engine embedded in application
• Multiple packaging options	
• Enterprise pricing, leverage infrastructure	• Toolkit packaging, OEM offering
• Services and SLA (service level agreement) orientation, minimizing risk	• Commodity oriented pricing, little added value
• Tools designed for site optimization and high accuracy	• Less consistent, lower performing product
• Real-time reporting with dynamic monitoring	• Fewer tuning options, less repeatable for multiple sites

Enterprise recognition evolved after financial institutions identified a variety of needs on how to:

1. Leverage hardware and software investments to reduce unit costs

2. Create a standardized platform of CAR/LAR with IQUA (image quality/usability) for consistent, superior results

3. Build a common support system for multiple applications

4. Reduce and eliminate a wide range of data-entry

requirements across multiple systems

The ultimate solution was to provide an on-demand recognition resource for unlimited applications, licensed so speed and distribution was not a limitation, with virtually 100 percent performance.

To meet customer objectives, Orbograph developed modules that run on the same hardware platform and are fully accessible to multiple check-processing applications simultaneously. For example, prime pass POD may be using [Centralized]IQUA for image quality and usability, while the RPS application is actively requesting recognition results from Accura CAR/LAR as the marketing group is running [Data]MindReader for marketing reports—all leveraging near 100 percent performance with APEX total automation.

In conclusion, a commodity-oriented product can provide lower initial investment levels than value-based solutions. However, the total cost of ownership is, on average, significantly lower with value-based, high-performance solutions.

11.5 Building Trust and Security into E-commerce Transactions
Steve Bohn, eCharge[2] Corporation

Protect yourself—and your customers—from Internet fraud with secure online payments.

E-commerce is an enabling process that promotes all industries globally over the Internet. Advances in broadband Internet access and wireless technology have created a new platform for Internet-enabled applications, allowing goods and services to be purchased and valuable information to be exchanged virtually between anyone, anytime, anywhere.

Unfortunately, the trust and security built into our traditional payment methods over many decades neither were designed for nor have kept pace with the new technology and business rules needed to support today's e-commerce transactions. As such, Web and e-mail services have quickly become the most common channels for criminals to initiate scams, and until consumers and businesses feel safe online, the economic foundations of the Internet—and billions of dollars of business worldwide—are at risk.

The Aberdeen Group staes that last year, 5.2 percent of online users reported that they had been victims of credit card fraud. Facing a problem that continues to grow exponentially with no effective solution currently available, Nashville-based eCharge[2] Corporation is poised to address what Aberdeen Group predicts could ignite a two trillion dollar global criminal industry by year end. Accordingly, Bill Gates predicted in the Wall Street Journal, "Technology companies that resolve the Internet-based-payment identity theft and fraud problems will be among the most successful companies in the public sector over the next ten years."

eCharge[2]'s early identification of this significant barrier to broad acceptance of Internet commerce led to the development of transformational technology that provides the only secure, fraud-free payment solution in the market. Committed to streamlining the payment services process in today's electronic society, eCharge[2]'s commercially tested, proven, and patent-pending products—PhoneAccount and NetAccount—safeguard your financial and confidential information while you make payments or transfer data over the Internet.

PhoneAccount is a secure and convenient online payment solution that allows businesses and consumers to purchase digital goods and services over the Internet and charge those purchases to their designated telephone, mobile phone, cable, Internet service provider or other utility bill. The PhoneAccount payment system eliminates the need to enter and exchange personal information (name, address, etc.) or sensitive financial information (credit card information, bank account numbers, etc.) over the Internet, creating a secure and private transaction environment.

NetAccount is a secure, real-time, fraud-free, online payment and cash management solution that allows users to manage credit, debit, prepaid, and stored-value account transactions with precise account management and control. Instead of exposing credit card or other bank account numbers and private user information, eCharge[2] utilizes digital certificates and its proprietary encryption technology to prevent fraud and ID theft from happening in the first place. Each transaction uses a unique three-way authentication process called "Triple Signature," which enables instantaneous validation and encryption of the multiple parties involved in every transaction (buyer, seller, and financial clearing partner or trusted third party) to transact business and payments over the Internet.

Major corporate partners, financial institutions, and payment processors will license PhoneAccount and NetAccount technologies to offer, under a "white-labeled" partner-distributor program, products and solutions that support their businesses, merchants, and consumer bases with a wide range of business-to-business, business-to-consumer, and person-to-person accounts and financial transactions.

To find out more about eCharge[2] Corporation and its products and services, please visit

www.echarge2.com or contact Steve Bohn, vice president of partners and alliances at 615-860-6240.

Chapter 12

Making Sense of Payments

Cathryn R. Gregg, Treasury Strategies, Inc.

At its most fundamental level, a payment is a means of transferring value. As straightforward as that is, the business of payments defies any simple categorization.

A few points illustrate the delightful complexity of this arena:

- Commercial banks have very distinct silos for credit card, retail, and corporate lines of business. Yet, payments interconnect all three.
- Payment forums tend to focus entirely on consumer transactions. Yet business payments issues have material impact on payment system changes.
- Many large participants in the broadly defined U.S. payments infrastructure have somewhat transparent management and control, as they are public and quasi-public entities. Yet there are also major players and influencers are closely controlled or private sector entities whose operations are much less transparent.

Numerous aspects of this delightfully complex market space are right now undergoing substantial transformation. Primary among these is the replacement of the paper check by any number of electronic and card alternatives.

No doubt, you remember the story of the blind men and the elephant. Each blind man felt a different part of the elephant and concluded something different—it was a tree (the leg), a snake (the trunk), and a wall (the stomach).

The U.S. payment system is quite similar today, which is why a book such as this makes interesting reading. This book includes chapters written from more than a dozen different perspectives. Although the authors are experts in their fields, it's still a challenge for anyone to feel they have a handle on where the payments system is going.

This chapter attempts to tie these perspectives together—to provide a better view of the elephant.

The Payments Context: Declining Check Volume

People intimately involved with payments know that a whole lot is going on all at once. People who are not intimately familiar may not notice most of the changes and may take those they do notice for granted. They simply alter their personal payment activities gradually over time as new options arise to fit their preferences and needs.

Many of us have done this; we have changed our personal payment activities. We now pay bills online. We allow some companies to debit our accounts. We pay with credit cards and debit cards. We use stored-value cards (like at Starbucks) and RDFI payment devices (including Mobil Speedpay and tollway passes). We have PayPal accounts.

To be sure, we still write checks—but far fewer of them. And the younger we are, the less likely we are to pay anything by check.

Corporations have also changed their payment activities. They pay electronically. They pay with purchasing cards. They issue payroll cards instead of payroll checks to employees without bank accounts. They use stored-value cards instead of handing out petty cash. To be sure, they still write checks—but fewer of them.

Experienced payment people are well aware of these trends. Yet, it is difficult to measure precisely how fast consumer and business checks are being swapped for electronic transactions. It is also difficult to project which substitute payment mechanisms will gain adequate critical mass to become institutionalized.

However, across all consumers and all corporations, check volume is down sufficiently so that our check-processing facilities now have substantial excess capacity. (Actual statistics are discussed in Chapter 7, "The Payment System Endgame.") Because so many banks have so much invested in the paper-check-processing model, this excess processing capacity has important bearing on the nature and rate of the evolution of payments systems.

Payments From 30,000 Feet

Over the years, the collective operators of the U.S. paper-check-clearing business made it a model of efficiency and low cost. But as paper check volumes decline, the average cost of clearing a check will rise if steps are not taken to cut capacity or other costs.

Thus, we have seen banks, the Federal Reserve, and clearing-houses doing radical surgery on the check-clearing infrastructure, closing and consolidating check-processing operations aggressively to eliminate excess capacity and keep costs down. This is not a one-time effort; as check volume keeps dropping, more surgery is required.

This leads to one of the more interesting debates in the payment space. To understand it, we need to separate the paper check process into two components: the "front end" (writing the paper check for payment) and the "back end" (clearing the paper check). What happens to one does not necessarily need to happen to the other. For example, the front end can remain paper, and the back end can be converted to an electronic format.

The debate is this: does it make sense to invest in improved efficiencies for the back end given that use of the front end is dwindling? Those who say no argue that a payment mechanism that will eventually all but disappear should not be the target of investment; it is onerous enough having to support the paper-clearing system as well as multiple alternatives while paper makes its slow descent into oblivion.Those who say yes then engage in a related debate that has to do with the best method of making the back-end process more efficient. A third debate deals with what mechanisms will most aggressively supplant the paper check as a front-end payment mechanism and thus also warrant investment.

Chapter 1, "Navigating New Waters," poses provocative questions around these debates. It asserts that we are in for a long transition until we reach a point where front-end paper check writing achieves a largely electronic state. However, the back-end process can be accomplished electronically now. This reality means the need for paper check *clearing* will plummet much more quickly than actual paper check *writing*.

This leads to speculation about how banks will manage clearing costs in an environment with low demand for the legacy paper-check-clearing infrastructure. One of the author's interesting ideas is that banks will reinstitute fees for paper checks (which have essentially been free for the last decade). Another interesting idea is that banks will collaborate and share processing facilities. The broad challenge is to minimize dollars directed at the legacy clearing system, dollars that could otherwise be directed toward investment in growing payment alternatives.

Chapter 7, "The Payment System Endgame," contends that checks are popular as a front-end payment vehicle for many reasons and will survive for a long time. The author offers a good explanation of how cost savings are being introduced to the back-end process through technology and newly permitted check-clearing and return paradigms. He assumes it makes sense for the industry to make these investments. His conclusion is that it is not necessary to encourage consumers or businesses to get rid of paper checks since clearing them is now so much more efficient.

For insight into the cost dynamics of back-office processing that have so radically changed with check volume declines, read Chapter 3, "Perspectives on Check". It is noteworthy that the author, a check operation manager for many years, credits much of the strength and integrity of the paper check system to trusted and well-understood rules and processes. He suggests that similar support for the full range of electronic payments is evolving and will be key to their eventual displacement of the paper check.

The New World

As mentioned above, the back-end process of paper check clearing is transforming. Almost every chapter in this book mentions Check 21, the legislation passed in 2003 that enabled much of this transformation. Check 21 permits electronic back-end check clearing via check image and gives legal status to a copy of the image.

Two chapters offer good reading on capabilities that have developed to support the post-Check 21 world. Check 21 eliminates the need for banks or their customers to physically transport checks to a central check-processing facility for deposit and clearing. Chapter 4, "A Short History of NetDeposit Inc,"discusses the origins of what has become known as remote deposit capture. This is one of the transformational technologies fueling the declining demand for paper-check-processing infrastructure.

Conceptually, remote deposit capture is the collection of protocols, software, and hardware that control what is now an electronic deposit and clearing process, a process that is driven off the image of the check rather than the actual paper document. In bringing the idea from conception to reality, each of these components presented challenges, which are artfully recounted in chapter 4.

Chapter 6, " Versatile Check Image Exchange", describes one approach to the last stage in the electronic back-end clearing process. Historically, bank transit functions coordinated physical clearing and transportation of checks through clearinghouses, direct presentments, and Fed presentments. Clearing arrangements were regularly optimized to minimize float and cost.

Electronic check clearing does not mean that clearing options instantly converge from many to one. Multiple clearing possibilities will persist, and not all options will be float neutral. Image exchange services address these and a host of new clearing challenges on behalf of their users. In so doing, they help advance the utility and accessibility of electronic check clearing of all types.

No discussion of payments is complete without considering how new payment mechanisms are displacing check writing or cash transactions. Most readers will be familiar with the extent to which ACH, credit card, and debit card payments have taken a prominent position in the payment system hierarchy. The Federal Reserve's often-cited 2004 study revealed that the volume of such payments (in aggregate) exceeded the volume of paper check payments for the first time.

Chapter 10, "Contactless Payments and the Credit Card (R)evolution," offers a glimpse into one of the more technologically chic payment types. Contactless payments involve a card or device that emits a radio-frequency signal. The signal receptor at the point of sale receives the signal, which contains all necessary identifier and account information to complete the transaction. For the most part, contactless payments replace cash transactions or the traditional credit-card swipe, rather than payments historically made with paper check, at the point of sale.

Payment Systems Background and Operations

Understanding the context in which payment change is occurring can be helpful in seeing the forest beyond the trees. Several chapters here shed light on how the U.S. payment system has gotten to where it is today. Some of them also offer insight into some payment system participants whose traditional behind-the-scenes roles are less commonly understood.

The author of Chapter 2, "Payments Observations," offers a half-century's history of modern-payment-system operations, having observed and understood them at close range. Anyone who appreciates that seemingly insignificant decisions and events can have ripple effects years later will find this chapter fascinating.

Along a similar vein, Chapter 9, "The Commercialization of the ACH," traces the evolution of one of the first broad-scale, non-payroll ACH applications. This and similar ACH applications built early consumer familiarity with this now-ubiquitous payment mechanism and helped establish its viability and robustness.

Clearinghouses are background players in the payments industry. Although they play a significant role, they are probably understood only by payments insiders. Chapter 5, "Check Clearing House Role in an Evolving Industry," describes how check clearinghouses came into being and evolved. Their settlement services, partnerships with other payment-system intermediaries, and role in payment-system risk management are all contributions to the smooth operation of the legacy paper-check-clearing system as well as today's evolving electronic exchanges.

Finally, for corporations, Check 21 creates the potential need for integrating yet another payment information stream into their receivables processes. Chapter 8, "Complex Payments," presents the viewpoint that, since such complexity is not going to diminish anytime soon, there is value in developing processing platforms that manage the blended paper and electronic payment streams.

Back to the Elephant

If they offer an opinion at all, the payment experts represented in this book conclude that paper check writing is here to stay for at least the intermediate term, albeit at diminished levels. Some are very interested in new technologies and processes to make back-end check clearing more efficient, and for them the logic is a foregone conclusion. Others are focused on check-displacement alternatives and building efficiencies in a world with multiple robust payment options.

Though they all touch a different part of the payments elephant, this seems appropriate. The tendency of our payment system transformation is obvious, but there is no clear timeframe or single direction that dominates. So it benefits us to have thoughtful experts and resources directed at a variety of reasonable possibilities.

Epilogue

The payments system—big as an elephant or an ocean—is immense. It's certainly impossible to examine it fully in a single written work. Even if it could be fully viewed or described in its current state, the system is complex, moving, and continually evolving. Our modest effort here was to share our experiences and give a bird's-eye view of what it has been and is—and perhaps mix in a little prophecy of what is to come.

Clearly, there are many payment channels to surf, with continuing waves of change ahead. The payments system will likely never be fully invented, understood, or perfected. It presents challenges and opportunities as infinite as the commerce it facilitates.

Most who read this book are adjusting to new payment options in their business and personal lives. Good information is essential to stay ahead of the curve and make wise decisions. Effective cash management can assure your success. Likewise, uninformed choices can negatively affect financial performance or even create significant loss.

Within these pages, I hope all readers find a new idea or information they'll find helpful in their own experiences "surfing payment channels."

Contributor Biographies

Rich Oliver

Rich Oliver is an executive vice president with the Federal Reserve Bank of Atlanta and has been with the bank since 1973.

Since 1998, he has served as retail payments product manager for the Federal Reserve system. In this capacity, he has responsibility for managing the Fed's check and ACH businesses nationwide.

Earlier in his career, Mr. Oliver served as planning analyst, administrator of the Automated Clearing House, chairman of the Federal Reserve's electronic payments implementation task force, manager and officer in charge of software development, vice president in charge of automation services, the Federal Reserve System's product manager for electronic payments services, officer in charge of business development and check software, and staff director for the Federal Reserve system's policy committee for financial services, where he was responsible for coordinating integrated financial management, project management, and strategic planning for all the Federal Reserve's payments services nationwide.

He also serves on the Federal Reserve Bank of Atlanta's management committee.

Jerry Milano

Jerry is the general manager of The Clearing House's national check services business with primary operations in seven of the ten largest U.S. metropolitan markets (New York, Los Angeles, Chicago, San Francisco, Boston, Philadelphia, and Detroit).

Prior to The Clearing House, Mr. Milano was president and CEO of the Western Payments Alliance (WesPay, 2000–2003), then the largest regional payments association in the U.S.;

president of Bankers Clearing House (1985–2000), then the largest check clearinghouse in the U.S.; president of the Chicago Clearing House (1982–1985); director of payments research and the payments system policy board at the American Bankers Association (1977–1982); and manager of retail banking systems at the First National Bank of Chicago, now JPM Chase (1967–1977).

Glenn Wheeler

Glenn Wheeler joined the NCHA in March 2002 and was named general manager in May 2006. In his leadership position, Glenn is directing NCHA's Check 21 and image initiatives, including developing partnership and alliances to best serve the changing needs of the industry. His primary responsibility is to manage the NCHA staff and to implement initiatives designed to be consistent with the NCHA's strategic direction. Included in that direction is the expansion of products and services that enable members to effectively address the shift from paper to image exchange—including issues related to check fraud, check fraud prevention, and changing risks resulting from the transition to image exchange.

Glenn joined NCHA from Bank One where he was an AVP and a manager in national float management. He was responsible for outbound national transportation, national clearinghouse strategy, and electronic check presentment implementations. Glenn previously worked for NCHA's predecessor organization, The Clearing House Association of the Southwest (CHAS).

Jeff Vetterick

Jeff Vetterick is general manager of Endpoint Exchange LLC, a Metavante company, which owns and operates the Endpoint Exchange Network, the country's first electronic-check-clearing network capitalizing on existing imaging infrastructure and settlement relationships, with the interoperability to connect to every endpoint in the nation. Vetterick oversees the sales and operations serving the financial institutions that join the Endpoint Exchange Network.

Prior to taking the leadership of Endpoint Exchange in 2005, Vetterick was vice president of marketing for Advanced Financial Solutions (AFS) and a member of its senior management team. Vetterick was responsible for providing leadership across all functional areas within AFS and for overseeing the strategic and market positioning of the company and its various software products for both internal and external audiences. A twenty-year veteran of the remittance and check-processing industry, Vetterick joined AFS in 1999 to launch the company's new enterprise document management division, which focused on developing page-centric imaging applications.

Before joining AFS, Vetterick was president of Panini North America, an Italian supplier of tabletop check sorting machines. Vetterick previously served as vice president of sales and marketing of the U.S. operations for Orbograph, an Israeli-based developer of check amount recognition software. Vetterick also held senior marketing and product management roles with Lundy Financial Systems, REI, and Banctec.

Vetterick has a bachelor of science degree in telecommunications from the University of Oregon. He is a frequent speaker on check payments at industry events and forums.

David Walker

Mr. Walker has more than eighteen years experience in data processing and twenty-five years in banking. He has worked with ECCHO since 1989 and currently serves as its president and CEO. Mr. Walker has worked with almost every aspect of the development and passage of the Check 21 Act since early 2000.

Prior to ECCHO, Mr. Walker held a senior management position with First RepublicBank, a predecessor bank of Bank of America, where he managed domestic and international wire transfer, ACH, cash concentration, and information reporting for all of the bank's Texas locations. Responsibilities also included IT for wire transfer and balance reporting, Fed Funds Trading, and Fed/Due From Position management. Mr. Walker also served as the bank's daylight overdraft coordinator and managed all daylight overdraft processes.

Mr. Walker also spent seven years with Electronic Data Systems Inc. in various positions including southeast regional operational manager with responsibility for nine locations across the southeast.

Mr. Walker is a graduate of the Southwestern Graduate School of Banking and earned a BA in economics from the University of Texas at Austin.

Robert F. Kirk

Bob Kirk has over twenty-five years of direct experience in financial services and cash management, along with extensive experience in executive management. Mr. Kirk joined VICOR in January 1999 as vice president of marketing. He was promoted to president and COO in 2002 and promoted to CEO in August of 2005. Under Bob's leadership at VICOR, the company's revenues and profitability have grown by more than 50 percent. Prior to joining VICOR, he was president of Enterprise Consulting Inc., where he consulted on a variety of strategic and operational aspects of the banking industry. Previously, he was vice president of marketing with BancTec Systems Inc., where he was responsible for marketing retail and wholesale remittance products. In addition, he was vice president of operations for Mellon Bank's nationwide lockbox operations. Bob holds bachelor's and master's degrees in business from West Virginia University and is a member of the board of directors of VICOR.

Mark A. Johnson

Mark A. Johnson is vice chairman of CheckFree Corporation, where he evaluates and marshals strategic growth opportunities for the company and develops strategic corporate relationships to support long-term business strategies. His primary focus is to expand CheckFree's opportunities in providing electronic services to a broader base of corporate and consumer customers. He is also a member of the CheckFree board of directors. Prior to joining CheckFree in the early 1980s, Johnson worked for the Federal Reserve Bank and Bank One. He currently serves as vice chairman of the Technology Association of Georgia Executive Committee and Board of Directors. He also serves on the board of directors for a number of private companies and is a member of the business advisory board of Miami University.

Mohammad Khan

Mohammad Khan is president and Founder of ViVOtech. Mohammad held several engineering, marketing, and business development management positions during the fifteen years he worked with VeriFone. After joining VeriFone in its early stage in 1983, Mr. Khan helped the company develop its payment automation systems and later helped successfully market these products in more than ninety-six countries. Included were the smart-card and security-payment products he conceived for VeriFone and launched to its worldwide markets in the early '90s. He was also a cofounder of the Internet commerce division within VeriFone and was responsible for expansion of its Internet payment systems business into more than twenty-five countries. Mr. Khan is a cofounder of Sparkice Inc., China's electronic hub for global commerce, where he worked as its senior vice president. He holds a master's degree in electrical engineering from the University of Hawaii at Manoa. In 2006 Khan was recognized as a leader of the Electronic Payments Industry by the Transaction Trends Magazine and in 2005 as a "Mover and Shaker" of the Electronic Payments Industry by the *Transaction World* magazine.

Cathryn R. Gregg

Cathy Gregg is a partner and director of Treasury Strategies Inc. She sets strategy and direction for the firm, leads the financial institution and corporate practices, and manages relationships and engagements with major banking and corporate clients. Ms. Gregg has pioneered approaches for payments business advancement in both the corporate treasury and banking sectors. She has focused on payment systems and banking industry evolution since founding the firm in 1982.

Ms. Gregg has been a keynote speaker at the Federal Reserve Bank of Chicago payments conference, NACHA, Tawpii, the AFP national conference, and numerous regional treasury and bank conferences. Prior to founding Treasury Strategies Inc., she had several years of experience at the First National Bank of Chicago, including work within their First Scholar program.

Ms. Gregg received her MBA from the University of Chicago following a BA in economics and psychology from Kenyon College, where she has served on the board of trustees. She is a permanently certified CCM and serves on the advisory boards of some of Treasury Strategies' bank clients. She has been the director of Marriage and Family Ministries and currently teaches women's studies at South Park Church. Cathy is also an avid gardener and cook.

Sponsoring Company Briefs

The Clearing House Payments Company

The Clearing House Payments Company (www.theclearing-house.org) is a private sector, global payment systems infrastructure that clears and settles twenty million payments for more than $1.5 trillion per day. The Clearing House serves more than 1,600 U.S. financial institutions and hundreds of international participants and manages payment services that span the entire spectrum of paper, paper-to-electronic, and electronic payments. Services include local and regional check exchange and settlement services, ACH association and operations, large-value 'wire' payments, electronic check presentment, and an image exchange. Financial institutions of all sizes benefit from payment systems that meet the highest standards for reliability, security, and service.

The Clearing House Payments Company is owned by the following banks or their U.S. banking affiliates: ABN AMRO Bank, Bank of America, The Bank of New York, Bank of Tokyo-Mitsubishi/Union Bank of California, BB&T, Citibank, Citizens Bank, City National Bank, Comerica Bank, Deutsche Bank, Fifth-Third Bank, HSBC Bank, JPMorgan Chase Bank, KeyBank, M&T Bank, National City Bank, PNC Bank, U.S. Bank, Wachovia Bank, and Wells Fargo Bank.

Originally established in 1851, The Clearing House is the oldest association of financial institutions in the United States. For more information on The Clearing House, contact chip.savidge@theclearinghouse.org or 212-613-9896.

Linx Payment Systems, LLC

Linx Payment Systems provides a variety of payment acceptance and billing related services, featuring Secure Payment Link, a single pay convenience option aimed at large billers to allow them to offer electronic payment choices to their clients in addition to traditional paper remittance alternatives. Secure Payment Link facilitates major credit card and e-check acceptance by Internet or telephone via fully automated secure Web sites and VRU (voice response unit) systems hosted and supported by top tier delivery and financial partners.

Other services include donation acceptance capability for non-profit organizations, e-billing notifications, automatic recurring payments, event registration support, merchant services, credit cards for business and personal use, consulting and various marketing services. For more information go to www.linxpay-mentsystems.com .

NetDeposit Inc.

NetDeposit Inc. was founded in 1999 and incorporated in January 2003 as a wholly-owned subsidiary of Zions Bancorporation.

Since then, NetDeposit has led the field in the development of image-based, distributed payment capture technology. NetDeposit was first to market with a corporate remote deposit capture platform, an image-based "decision gateway" for sorting and routing electronic items, and industrial-grade image replacement document (IRD) print software. This technology has matured over several generations of development and through direct feedback from NetDeposit customers.

For over four years, NetDeposit technology has enabled remote capture and electronic clearing and currently powers the nation's top IRD print networks. NetDeposit solutions have processed millions of electronic items. NetDeposit offers its technology for licensed, in-house deployments and through an on-demand, hosted service.

NetDeposit Inc. delivers the power and promise of check electronification to financial institutions, third-party processors, and corporations. NetDeposit's NetCapture, NetConnect, and NDpro solutions help financial institutions leverage the new marketplace enabled by Check 21 legislation by facilitating the remote capture, sorting, and routing of electronic items. Since its founding in 1999, NetDeposit solutions have powered thousands of remote capture locations and processed millions of electronic items.

NetDeposit is a subsidiary of Zions Bancorporation (NASDAQ: ZION). For information, call 801-273-6067, send e-mail to info@ netdeposit.com, or visit www.netdeposit.com.

The National Clearing House Association

The National Clearing House (NCHA) is the single-largest settler of clearinghouse check volume in the United States, settling more than 6.7 billion items annually. A member-owned and member-driven national association of financial institutions, NCHA provides check clearing, settlement, risk management, and related services to 709 check-processing sites representing 539 financial institutions and provides settlement and related services for 20 customer clearinghouses across the country. NCHA is the only organization of its kind that provides settlement services for all types of transactions (ECP, checks, images, manual entries, and manual adjustments) in a single application. NCHA provides a standardized platform and standardized rules and has been recognized as the leader of settlement activities and the gateway to all major providers of both check and image services, including the top 20 banks in the nation, allowing its constituents the ability of choice.

NCHA supports all industry standards and continues to expand services through valuable partnerships and alliances in its commitment to provide risk management-related services, promote image exchange, and assist the industry in the transition from paper to electronic clearing. Visit NCHA on the Web at www.TheNCHA.com.

Endpoint Exchange Network

The Endpoint Exchange Network enables U.S. financial institutions to clear their check-based transactions by exchanging check images between member institutions. The Endpoint Exchange

Network (www.endpointexchange.com) is the country's first electronic-check-clearing network that capitalizes on existing imaging infrastructure and settlement relationships, with the interoperability to connect to every endpoint in the nation. Metavante Corporation (www.metavante.com) is a leading provider of image-based check processing and distributed image-capture solutions, which include the Endpoint Exchange Network. Metavante delivers banking and payment technologies to financial services firms and businesses worldwide and is wholly owned by Marshall & Ilsley Corporation (NYSE: MI).

Electronic Check Clearing House Organization (ECCHO)

ECCHO is a national clearinghouse that is owned by its member depository financial institutions. Created in 1990, ECCHO has five hundred members and provides rules for the exchange of check images. ECCHO's members hold more than 60 percent of the total U.S. deposits.

ECCHO coordinated the Industry Group, which included more than 140 individuals representing more than 60 organizations including banks, credit unions, banking trade associations, technology companies, and other clearinghouses. The Industry Group created consensus positions and recommendations to the Federal Reserve and the U.S. Congress relative to the Check 21 Act. ECCHO was involved in virtually every aspect of the passage of Check 21.

ECCHO's primary functions are image exchange rules, education, and industry advocacy. Rules are needed for image exchange because check image exchange is not addressed in statutory, regulatory, or case law.

VICOR Inc. A Metavante Company

VICOR Inc. is the leading provider of solutions that optimize the processing of complex payments for businesses and financial institutions. By managing multiple payment types and formats across diverse distribution channels, VICOR helps businesses and financial institutions save time and money, attract new customers, generate revenue, and leverage existing technologies. VICOR serves the following market segments: receivables, Check 21, government forms processing, payables, healthcare, and B2B e-payments. In 2005, VICOR's solutions processed over $1.4 trillion in payment volume, 222 million payment transactions, and 335 million payment-related documents. VICOR owns and manages the Corporate Payment Progress Index (CPPI), an industry initiative that quantitatively measures the progress of corporate payments. VICOR is headquartered in Richmond, CA.

CheckFree Corporation

Founded in 1981, CheckFree Corporation (Nasdaq: CKFR) provides financial electronic commerce services and products to organizations around the world. CheckFree Electronic Commerce solutions enable thousands of financial services providers and billers to offer their customers the convenience of receiving and paying their household bills online or in person through retail outlets. CheckFree Investment Services provides a broad range of investment management solutions and outsourced services to thousands of financial services organizations, which manage about $1.3 trillion in assets. CheckFree Software develops markets and supports software applications that are used by financial institutions to process more than two-thirds of the twelve billion Automated Clearing House transactions in the United States. The division also provides operational risk management, financial messaging, corporate actions, and regulatory compliance software to more than 1,500 organizations across the globe.

ViVOtech

ViVOtech is the market leader in contactless/NFC payment software, transaction management systems, and readers. These innovative solutions allow consumers to make contactless payments with radio frequency-enabled credit cards, debit cards, key fobs, and NFC-enabled mobile phones. ViVOtech's products are used by some of the most prominent retailers in the United States. Currently, with more than 200,000 units in 18 countries, ViVOtech's products are in use at movie theaters, fast food restaurants (QSR), casual dining establishments, convenience stores, gas stations, drug stores, grocery stores, buses, taxicabs and vending machine locations, enabling a wide variety of businesses to accept contactless/NFC payments. In 2005, ViVOtech received the prestigious Frost & Sullivan technology award for its role in transforming the contactless payment industry, as well as winning the first annual ETA Technology Innovation Award. http://www. vivotech.com.

Treasury Strategies Inc.

Founded in 1982, Treasury Strategies Inc. is a client-focused management consulting firm serving corporations and financial institutions. As a thought leader in treasury, liquidity, payments, and working capital management, Treasury Strategies develops customized and actionable solutions unparalleled in the marketplace. For more information, visit our Web site at www. TreasuryStrategies.com .

Additional View Contributions

Clint Shank
SortLogic Systems
A Division of Omni-Soft Inc
www.SortLogic.com

Wally Vogel
Creditron
www.creditron.com

Gary Provo
Executive Vice President
eGistics, Inc
214-256-4613
gprovo@egisticsinc.com
www.egisticsinc.com

Joseph J. Gregory
Vice President, U.S. Operations
Orbograph
An Orbotech Company
978-901-5042
joe.gregory@orbograph.com
www.orbograph.com

Steven G. Bohn
Vice President-Partners and Alliances
eCharge² Corporation
615-860-6240
sbohn@echarge2.com
www.echarge2.com

Index